By Leaps and Bounds

C. GARY ROPER, Ph.D., and
JUDITH H. DEMAREST

By Leaps and Bounds

□ ◆ □

*A Parents' Guide to
Measuring Child Development,
Ages 3 to 5*

Illustrations by Nancy Sarama

An Owl Book
Henry Holt and Company | New York

*We deeply appreciate the assistance of Fred Rapczynski,
research associate and staff school psychologist,
in the preparation of this book.
His advice has been invaluable.*

Published by Henry Holt and Company, Inc.,
521 Fifth Avenue, New York, New York 10175.
Distributed in Canada by Fitzhenry & Whiteside Limited,
195 Allstate Parkway, Markham, Ontario L3R 4T8.

Library of Congress Cataloging-in-Publication Data
Roper, C. Gary.
By leaps and bounds.
"An Owl Book."
Includes index.
1. Child development. 2. Child development—Testing.
3. Parenting. I. Demarest, Judith H. II. Title.
HQ767.9.R64   1986   649'.1   86-4745
ISBN 0-8050-0347-9

First Edition

Designed by Victoria Hartman
Printed in the United States of America
10 9 8 7 6 5 4 3 2 1

ISBN 0-8050-0347-9

For our own boundless leapers—Alison, Jane, Katie, and Kevin—whose preschool years we remember so fondly.

Contents

tion in this area, and what parents can do to help the child develop these skills.

10 | Gauging Personality   205

Games and tests to help parents grasp the patterns of behavior that make up their own distinctive offspring. A special section on what parents can do if their child needs special attention in this area.

Appendix A. Case Histories and Conclusions   223

Appendix B. Tests   245

Measures frequently used by professionals for screening or assessment of preschoolers.

Glossary   248

Selected Bibliography   255

Index   257

By Leaps and Bounds

Introduction

This book is for every mother who cannot resist comparing her preschooler to other youngsters; for every father who has ever asked himself, "Are all kids like this?"; for every parent who has wondered, "Where can we go for help?"

It's a book for parents who are beginning to realize that their child is very bright, and that they have a responsibility to help him achieve his full potential.

It's a book for parents who are beginning to think that their child might have a particular problem, and that she will need some special help to achieve her full potential.

It's a book for parents whose children are well within the range we call "normal" or "average" who want to help their children achieve their full potential.

It's a book for all parents who worry and think and care about their children.

Parents must give up their autonomy when it comes to raising kids within a community and a school system. Although mothers and fathers bear the primary responsibility for raising the child and coping with any special situations that arise, it is the school or the medical community that does the testing and evaluating—and makes the decisions as to whether and when these tests will be performed. Through intimate knowledge of their child, parents may intuit that Peter or Katie requires special handling, whether because of superior abilities or because of certain disabilities. Most parents, however, lack three essential tools for making these special conditions known and for dealing with them: specific experience, specific language, and specific knowledge.

Very few parents have the experience with the variety of children that would enable them to understand what constitutes "normal" childhood behavior. It's not enough to have been a child once, many years past. (Life is not what it used to be, even twenty years ago. It's faster now, packed with more stimuli, more choices, more conflicts, and, in defiance of natural law, less time. Being a kid is tougher now than it was then. And in spite of the fact that more child-rearing information is available to parents these days, being a parent is tougher, too.)

It's not enough, either, to have raised a child—or even several children. In order to understand the full range of normal behavior, it helps to have observed hundreds of childhoods—and few parents can have had that opportunity. Lacking this broad experience, parents may wonder, "Sarah can say her alphabet, and she's not even three. Does that make her a genius?" Or "Matt's four, and he can't get it together on his brother's bike. Will he always be such a klutz?" Or "Shouldn't Jamie be able to hold his head up now that he's three months old?" Some of these concerns may be baseless; some may be well-founded—but the parents may lack the experience to determine which is which.

Many parents also lack the language necessary to communicate the reasons for their concern. A mother may say to the pediatrician, "Jenny doesn't seem to be as quick as Georgie was at six months," and the pediatrician, who has been hearing this from overconcerned parents for years, may say, "Now, Mother, don't worry. Every child develops according to his own schedule." That same pediatrician, when told that "Jenny doesn't track objects with her eyes when I move them across her field of vision" might suggest that Jenny's sight be tested more thoroughly.

Finally, in this world of specialists, many parents lack knowledge of where to head for help. They might, for instance, consult a neurologist for their daughter's headaches, but it might not occur to them to see what help a psychologist can offer.

This book can help you answer the questions you may be asking yourself—the questions schools and doctors may someday ask you. It will help you to determine if or when your child's behavior falls outside the range of "normal" behavior. It will help you to gather some basic information about your child, consult the proper specialists, and communicate in language that will make your concern clear.

HOW THIS BOOK IS DIFFERENT

This is not a "test your child's IQ" book. The IQ test can be a helpful tool in determining a child's status in relationship to that of other children; but the IQ test, or any other single test taken by itself, can't be very meaningful. To focus in too closely on one small part of a child's functioning is like trying to judge a child's looks by the shape of his ears—it's misleading. The aim of this book is to help you keep your whole child in view.

Neither is this an armchair diagnosis book. It won't—can't—tell you what is wrong with your child. You will not find here a list of symptoms to convince you that your child has Tourette's syndrome or *grand mal* epilepsy. Instead, we will indicate the range of behavior that is normal and suggest that if a child falls consistently outside that range, there are certain consultants who might be able to offer help and concrete information.

This book won't tell you not to worry, or not to compare your child to other children. Parents *do* worry. You *do* compare. It is our intention to help you compare on the basis of reliable experience and information, and then—if there really might be something to worry over—to do something about it.

This isn't a "how to raise your child" book, either. There are plenty of excellent books available that offer child-rearing suggestions. We've listed some in our bibliography. We're not attempting to duplicate or replace these books.

This is not a solutions book. It's a "do" book, requiring action on your part. We can show you how to gather information about your child; we can help you determine for yourself where your child lies within—or outside—the broad range of normality. We can help you decide what to do next. We can't diagnose your child with this book, and neither can you. That can be done only in consultation with competent professionals.

With the information in this book, you will be able to make your own informed decisions about your child. You'll have a basis for comparing your child that is broader and more accurate than the performance of the kid next door.

It is not our intention to help or encourage you to accept or assign blame for any problems your child may be experiencing. In fact, our intention is the opposite. Your child is on a pathway of development. You need to know where on that path she is, but you cannot totally change the path. What you can do is to help your child along the path, reduce frustration and disappointment, and see that she takes no unnecessary turns.

FORMAT OF THIS BOOK

The book begins with several chapters on the subject of tests and testing to provide background information and some basic instructions on the best way to play the games and conduct the tests. Then comes a chapter briefly reviewing the progress a child can be expected to make from infancy through five years of age.

The tests. The tests and observations are grouped into chapters covering self-help skills, learning and general information, motor skills, visual and auditory perception, language skills, cognitive skills, and personality. The tests, developed by the authors and based on wide experience in working with children of all types, are face-value observational measurements, easily conducted by parents. They are not normed, commercial tests requiring training, practice, and minute accuracy in scoring. A child will not "pass" or "fail" these tests. He will simply be rated as high, midrange, or low.

Scoring. Although the tests are not numerically scored, each test area will indicate the child's broad-range performance: average, above average, or below average.

Evaluation. After the tests in each chapter, there will be a section on evaluating the results of the tests. Here you will discover whether your child falls within the range of normality or is above or below normal.

Follow-up. At the end of each group of related tests, there will be a discussion of the various types of specialists who may be consulted for more information if you suspect that a problem exists. We have also presented some concrete suggestions for increasing your child's capacity in each area—whether your child is of high, low, or average ability in that particular skill.

Survey of tests. Included in this section will be a listing and short descriptions of the tests that schools and the medical community may perform on children aged three to five.

Glossary. Included in this section will be a list of the common terms that relate to child growth and development in this age group.

Why Measure Your Child's Growth and Development?

Chances are that somewhere in your bookshelves, or tucked away in a drawer, you have a "baby book." When your child was born, you began filling in the pages, keeping track of the first smile, the first tooth, the first step—recording the progress you all made during that challenging, rewarding first year.

And chances are that before the end of the second year, you stopped making entries in the baby book.

After all, once you've noted the first word and the first sentence and the first dry night, what else is there to record?

Plenty. And this book is the place to do it.

This book is full of games, observations, checklists, and tests that you and your child can do together, and spaces to record the results.

Some of you may be saying, "Tests? What business does a parent have testing a child? Parents are supposed to love and guide their children, not test them!"

We agree that parents are supposed to love and guide. But loving and guiding are easier when you understand your child. And with the games, observations, checklists, and, yes, tests in this book, you can gain a greater understanding of your young bundle of inconsistencies. The information you will record in this book will be as absorbing and as useful as the notes on the first day Kevin drank from a cup or managed to get most of a spoonful of beans into his mouth. Because with these measuring devices, you can watch your child grow and learn.

And *you'll* learn, too. You'll learn who your Kevin is and what he's capable of and how you can help him to grow and learn more and better.

Because it's not the level Kevin has reached that tells the story—it's the progress he has made. Growth is invisible at any single point. Progress—up or down—is an action that can only be measured by some sort of systematic observation at different points in time. One mark on the door measuring your child's height does not show growth. It's that second mark two inches higher a year later that tells the real growth story.

If you go out to your garden and look at the flowers poking up in the early spring, you'll see the tips of tulips and daffodils, each showing just an inch or so above the ground. You can tell by looking at them which is poking up higher, but if you wanted to say which grows faster, you would have to measure them. Let's say the tulips are one and a half inches and the daffodils are one inch high. You wait for a period of time and check again. This time you find differences. Perhaps the daffodil shoots are up to three and a half inches while the tulips are now two inches. Now it is clear that the daffodils, while smaller to begin with, were growing faster and, in fact, are bigger now. Determining how fast something develops, whether it's flowers or children, depends on measurement over time. Without the first measurement, there is no basis on which to compare—and yet the single measurement alone can't tell much about growth and change. These first measurements may allow a teacher or psychologist who tests your child to see *growth*, not just the child's present level of functioning.

This book will introduce you to the art of systematic observation of your child's everyday activities, and to special techniques that will help you to measure and record progress. As you watch, you'll become alert to the changes your child undergoes. And you'll come to see these changes as a meaningful, orderly unfolding—sometimes subtle, sometimes obvious, and always amazing.

The games and observations in this book will also help you to do something your pediatrician has probably told you not to do, something that you do anyway, with varying degrees of guilt and furtiveness: compare your child to other children.

It's a natural part of loving your child. When Rachel next door learns to tie her shoes at the age of four and a half, you watch your five-year-old struggle, and you wonder, "Is Rachel ahead of her time, or is Kevin slow?" And when Kevin learns to spell his name while Rachel is still working on capital R, Rachel's mother is probably wondering the same thing. She can't help comparing and wondering, any more than you can. It's only human to be concerned—and curious.

Here's another good reason for playing our games: They're fun! This is your chance to sit down with your kid and have a good time. You'll both have fun while you watch your child grow. (Perhaps we should say "children," because it's fun and instructive to play the games with all of your children, not just the first.)

Kevin will be glad, when he reaches adulthood, to have the games, drawings, and checklists in this book as a record of his growing years, or you can keep the book to show to your grandchildren as *they* grow up: "Look at Daddy's first house picture!"

So you can test Kevin to watch him learn and grow; you can test to satisfy your curiosity; you can test for the fun of it. And there's one more reason for testing your child: Early testing and observation on a consistent, regular basis can help to detect significant variations from that broad range of behaviors and abilities that we call "normal." By using these measuring devices, you may be able to catch on quickly if Kevin falls consistently into the above-normal range—so you can encourage his progress. And if he consistently has trouble in some areas, you may also spot that quickly so you can check into the possibility of having a professional evaluation done to detect any long-term problems.

Detection of problems can be of crucial importance to a child's growth and development in many areas. But real children grow in complex and ever-changing ways. The longer a problem exists, the more complex it may become. A close look at the story of Jason will show many typical problems parents may encounter.

Jason's Story

Jason Evans was an easy baby right from the start. Barbara thoroughly enjoyed this, her second pregnancy; the birth was quick, uncomplicated, and one day early. "Jason has a better record for on-time deliveries than the post office," Mike Evans joked.

"And what a difference from Lisa!" Barbara added. "Two weeks old, and he's already sleeping through the night!"

Mike laughed. "Lisa sure was a beaut! Remember we had to drive her around in the car for an hour every night to get her to go to sleep? Good thing we don't have to do that with him—November's too cold for it."

"And no colic with Jason, either. Looks like number two is a worry-free baby."

"We get better with practice," Mike teased.

Jason continued to be a pleasure. He stayed on a consistent sleep schedule and was a happy, good-natured infant. Even when his first teeth came in at six months, he showed only mild irritability; a frozen teething ring usually soothed the congested gums and brought back the smiles.

He took his first steps at ten months on a hot September afternoon by the swimming pool. "Well, there goes my peace of mind," Barbara joked, scooping him up and carrying him away from the water.

A few weeks before his first birthday, Jason said his first word. "I couldn't believe it," Barbara reported to Mike that evening. "Here we've been trying for weeks to get him to say 'Mama' or 'Daddy,' and then suddenly he just walks up to me and says 'Hi!' "

By the time Jason was eighteen months old, Barbara had to tie the knobs of the kitchen cabinets together to keep him from opening them. He was full of curiosity and the spirit of exploration. Whatever was in something had to come out; whatever was on something had to come off; whatever was up had to come down.

He could feed himself with a spoon, and he made valiant attempts to hold his glass with two hands. His favorite toys were his blocks and a small rubber ball. Mostly he just pushed them around the floor, but sometimes, when the mood struck, he could stack all of three blocks. Lisa usually pushed them over, and he would giggle and stack them up again.

At this point, Jason began to show an interest in what went on in the bathroom. He would stalk manfully up to the toilet, diapers and all, and stand in front of it, belly out. "Like Daddy doos," he would comment in great satisfaction.

Taking advantage of his interest, Barbara started toilet training him, and when he turned two years and three months, she could sail past the disposable diapers in the supermarket without a second glance.

"Boy, we must be doing something right," Mike said. "We've got two terrific kids, and they're both smart as whips. Let's do it again!"

Barbara's third pregnancy was not as easy as her second. She tired easily and found herself losing her temper even with easygoing Jason. Lisa was in nursery school, and she brought home new germs every week. It seemed to Barbara that either Lisa or Jason was constantly suffering from coughs and colds—especially Jason, whose illnesses always seemed to linger longer than Lisa's. His entire second year was one long battle with his runny nose. "If I blow one more nose, or find one more wad of soggy Kleenex in my pocket, I'm going to move into a home for retired mothers," Barbara told the pediatrician—and she was only half joking.

"Does Jason complain when he's sick?" Dr. Brumley asked, thumping the little bare back.

"No—he's an angel."

"Well, I wouldn't worry. A string of colds like this is very common when older brothers or sisters start school." Dr. Brumley wrote out a prescription for a decongestant and told Barbara to use it until the cold was gone.

Evening storytime became something of a trial to Barbara. She was seven months pregnant, and it was hard to fit two children on what was left of her lap—particularly when Jason started to wiggle.

"He just isn't as interested in stories as Lisa was at his age," Barbara complained to her mother. "What should I do?"

"Lisa's books are too old for him," her mother said. "He should be learning nursery rhymes at this age."

So Barbara went back to the nursery rhymes that Jason had once loved, and that he knew so well that he would give her the last word in every line. But these old favorites couldn't hold his attention either, and gradually Barbara stopped trying to read to him.

Richard was born a month before Jason's third birthday. He was a demanding baby; for three months Barbara carried him with her everywhere but to the bathroom. Looking back, she was sure that this period marked some kind of turning point for Jason. From the happy, pleasant little boy he had been, Jason became uncooperative and indifferent—even irritable.

"Boy, Jason's really getting to be a pain," she told Mike one evening. "I called and called him to come in today, and I finally had to go out and drag him in, kicking and screaming all the way. You'd have thought I was the Lord High Executioner coming to do him in! Oh, and he actually pinched Richard this afternoon. It's really not like him to be so rotten."

"Lay off the poor kid," Mike said. "It's just sibling rivalry. He's going through a bad patch. He'll get over it."

"That's easy for you to say—you don't have to cope with him all day," Barbara muttered, but she was reassured, nonetheless.

In September, a few months before Jason's fourth birthday, Barbara enrolled him in the same nursery school Lisa had attended. The first few weeks were unexpectedly difficult—Jason cried and carried on when Barbara tried to leave him at the school. Miss Genualdi, his teacher, reported that he usually settled down within a few minutes, but that he seemed "kind of shy." "He doesn't join in with the group much," she said. "Has he always been a loner?"

"No, not at all," Barbara answered, surprised. "He's always had lots of friends in the neighborhood. What do you think the problem is?"

"Oh, I'm sure there's no problem. Lots of kids take a bit of time to get used to the school atmosphere."

However, the week after Jason's fourth birthday, in November, Miss Genualdi caught Barbara as she dropped Jason off and asked to speak to her.

"Nothing serious," she said. "I just wanted to let you know that Jason sometimes seems to be kind of cranky with the other kids and a little uncooperative with the teachers. He's often the last one to stop playing at Circle Time, and he has to be called more than once."

Barbara went home worried. She began to watch Jason closely, but he seemed pretty much himself—his new self, that is. The old sunny Jason had apparently gone forever.

Mike refused to be concerned. "How old is Miss Genualdi—fifty-five? And never had a kid of her own? She sounds like a typical old fussbudget to me. Know what Jason told me today? He said 'Miss Gennywally looks like a witch when she frowms.' Do all the kids call her that?"

"No—just Jason. Did he really say 'frowm'?"

Mike chuckled. "Yeah."

"He really doesn't speak as clearly as Lisa did at that age."

"Oh, for crying out loud, Barb, you're as bad as Miss Gennywally! All kids mispronounce words sometimes. It's part of being a kid—one of the cute parts!" Mike had to raise his voice to make himself heard as Jason turned on the TV in the next room.

Barbara could feel the tension up her back. "Jason, turn that TV down! How many times do I have to tell you?" she shouted. Then she felt guilty for yelling at Jason when it was really Mike she was annoyed at.

At the end of January, when it was conference time at the nursery school, Miss Genualdi again mentioned that Jason had been increasingly uncooperative and irritable, lashing out at the other children for no reason anyone could discover. Delicately, the teacher led up to her question: "Have there been any—difficulties—at home? Any problems in the family?"

Searching her mind, Barbara confessed that there had been some economic problems. "Money is always tight, but right now it seems to be tighter than ever—and with three kids—but we never talk about it in front of the children."

Miss Genualdi smiled patiently. "You know, children often react to stresses in their parents' lives, even when the parents don't think they're showing any stress. Might I suggest that you and your husband seek professional counseling?"

Stunned, Barbara reported the conversation to Mike. Mike hit the roof.

"If you think I'm going to trot off to a shrink on the advice of some dried-up old crone—what does she think, that we're *crazy*? Let me tell you something: this is a typical, happy family, damn it! There's nothing wrong with us. It's that *school* that's causing the problems! Get him out of there!"

Barbara didn't know what to do. It didn't seem to her that she and Mike had any real problems. But Miss Genualdi had had so many years of experience—surely she would know when the problem was serious enough to require outside help.

On the other hand, Dr. Brumley, who had been seeing Jason regularly since birth, had never mentioned any abnormalities or changes in the boy.

Confused and not knowing where to turn, Barbara called the pediatrician for an appointment to discuss Jason's problem.

Dr. Brumley was kind enough to see Barbara quickly, sandwiching her in between appointments. Conscious that he was a busy man, Barbara hurried through her story. "Do you think we should go to a psychiatrist?" she finished nervously.

"Miss Genualdi probably meant a psychologist, not a psychiatrist," Dr. Brumley said soothingly. "And no, I really don't think that seems appropriate."

Barbara was about to ask what the difference was between a psychiatrist and a psychologist when the phone on the doctor's desk rang. He answered it tersely and said, "I'll be there as soon as I can."

Feeling guilty at taking up his time with her problems, Barbara quickly left.

After several long discussions, the Evanses decided that, rather than making a change in Jason's life right now, when he was having problems adjusting, they would leave him at the nursery school.

By early spring, school reports indicated that Jason was falling behind the other children in his group, especially in language development.

"Is he the lowest in the class?" Barbara asked apprehensively.

"Oh, no, no. Not at all," Miss Genualdi answered. "But I believe he is capable of much more. He's not keeping up with our expectations—or his own self-expectations. And he's getting more and more frustrated.

He doesn't seem to enjoy our activities anymore. It's like he's just going through the motions."

Barbara responded to this situation by trying to spend more time with Jason. The only effect this had was to make Jason dependent on her and cranky when she had to spend time away from him.

When Jason was four and a half, another option became available. He was now eligible to enter public kindergarten starting in September. But Miss Genualdi advised against it.

"I don't think it would be a good idea to put Jason through the pre-kindergarten screening program at this point," she said. "It would be setting him up for failure, and he doesn't need another failure right now. He doesn't do well in a testing situation, and I really feel he'd be better off if you left him here for one more year."

Barbara wasn't surprised when Mike objected to this idea. She realized that it was hard for Mike to bear the thought that his son might be slower than other children his age. But it wasn't easy for her to bear, either, and she wished Mike would offer some sort of constructive alternative instead of just arguing with everything the professionals said. She was beginning to feel caught in the middle, with no idea where to turn for help. In desperation, and in defiance of Miss Genualdi, she called the elementary school and described the situation to the principal over the telephone.

"I think you should bring him in for the preschool screening," Mrs. Rivera said. "I'll be able to tell you more definitely what should be done after I've seen Jason. You know, this screening isn't really a test—it's a get-acquainted session, so we can discover each child's potential capabilities. Jason can't possibly 'fail.' "

Barbara brought Jason to the screening program in the elementary school gym during the last week in May. She sat in a child-size blue chair at the edge of the floor with a group of other mothers and watched Jason and several other boys and girls go through the screening program. They walked along a two-by-four, tossed some beanbags, did some drawing, worked on some puzzles, and were seen in private interviews by the principal, the school nurse, the school psychologist, the kindergarten teacher, and the speech and hearing specialist.

Barbara watched Jason and the other children carefully. Was he slower than the others? Faster? The same? She really couldn't decide. He seemed to be less physically adept at some things—walking the two-by-four was particularly hard for him—but he solved the puzzles much faster than the other children she had observed. What did it mean?

The next day she got a call from the school nurse.

"We'd like you to bring Jason in for further evaluation, Mrs. Evans. We haven't found any specific problems, but Jason does seem somewhat immature."

"What does that mean?" Barbara asked.

"Well, November birthday boys are often developmentally behind their peer norm group," the nurse answered patiently.

Barbara still did not feel fully informed, but she hesitated to display her ignorance by asking again, so she made the appointment to take Jason in for re-evaluation.

A week or so after this second evaluation, Barbara received another call from the school. The speech and hearing specialist had been unable to get a complete screening on Jason, for reasons Barbara didn't understand, and wanted to see him again. Barbara set up another appointment, a bit wearily. But when the day came, she had to reschedule it for another day: Jason had one of his ear infections.

"All these appointments and tests and screenings," Barbara complained to her neighbor, "and I still don't even know if anything is really wrong. Maybe Miss Genualdi is right. Maybe I should just keep him in nursery school for another year."

Her neighbor nodded. "You know, Danny was an October birthday boy, and I kept him out of kindergarten until he was almost six. I really think it was the best thing I ever did. He was the oldest and the smartest kid in his class, and he really responded to that. He's doing fantastic this year."

Thinking it over, Barbara decided to skip the rescheduled speech and hearing session. She would do what Danny's mother had done—hold Jason back and put him in kindergarten next year. She called the school to cancel the appointment.

"Oh, Mrs. Evans, I really think you should bring Jason in for the speech and hearing evaluation," the nurse said. "If you want to delay entering him in school, you can make that decision anytime, but it can't hurt to have all the information before you finally decide."

And Barbara, recognizing the logic of that, agreed to bring Jason in for evaluation.

Late in June, the Evanses received a letter from the speech and hearing specialist. "Our tests indicate delayed language development and mild articulation problems. The audiological screening was inconclusive. Please call the school for an appointment to discuss these findings."

"What's an audiological screening?" Mike demanded. Barbara shrugged and made the appointment. Maybe this time she'd get some answers.

But as it turned out, all she got was more questions—and suggestions for more appointments.

"Given Jason's previous history of adjustment difficulty and the background of family problems, we suggest a battery of psychological tests," the school nurse said.

"Family problems? What family problems?"

"Jason's nursery-school teacher indicated that there was some tension between you and your husband. Family counseling might help us all to determine the root of Jason's problems."

Barbara was noncommittal—but when she told Mike about it, she was indignant. "Where did they get the idea that we have family problems? How do these things get blown out of proportion? I tell Miss Genualdi that money is tight, and all of a sudden they think we're heading for the divorce court."

"So what was the upshot?" Mike asked.

"The upshot is that they think Jason is perfectly capable of entering kindergarten this fall. They said they'd do the psychological tests in September when the school year begins."

To Barbara's pleased surprise, Jason took the first day of school in his stride. There were no tears when she dropped him off. He and his best friend went off to class with the others in their group, and Barbara stopped in at the principal's office to ask about the psychological tests.

Mrs. Rivera was busy, but she was pleased to see Barbara. "The first few weeks of school are always hectic, but as soon as things settle down a bit, Jason will be picked up for testing. We'll be sure to let you know."

September passed, and Barbara had heard nothing from the teacher or the school. "What's up?" Mike asked.

"Well, I guess as long as we don't hear, everything must be going all right," Barbara answered.

In mid-October, the school held its open house for parents. Mike and Barbara both went, anxious to meet Jason's teacher and get a fix on how things were going.

Mrs. Berquist, however, was surrounded by other parents, all equally anxious to meet the teacher and find out how their children were getting along. "I haven't got time to go over everything with you right now, but I do want to talk to you. Can you come in after school on Wednesday?" she asked. Barbara agreed.

On Wednesday, Mrs. Berquist laid it on the line.

"Jason seems to be a bright child, but he has a short attention span. He's very restless, always shifting around in his seat or walking around the class disturbing other students. He has difficulty following directions, and he gets frustrated very easily when things don't go the way he wants. He's often loud and rambunctious at inappropriate times, and socially, he's just not well adapted. He's got the ability to be a good student, but he's not using it!"

By the end of this summary, Barbara was almost in tears. "What can we do?"

"I'd recommend psychological testing, for a start," the teacher said gently.

"But Jason was supposed to have started psychological testing right here in the school last month! The principal has already recommended it!"

Mrs. Berquist was surprised to hear this, and she said she would remind the principal to send in a referral for Jason's psychological testing.

Two weeks later, the school psychologist called to say that he needed

Mike and Barbara to sign a parental permission form, and that he'd mail one to the Evanses' home.

"Why didn't they tell us this months ago?" Mike grumbled.

Two weeks later, no permission form had arrived. Barbara called the psychologist, who told her that the form was in the mail. Four days later, it finally arrived.

By now it was the beginning of December. Jason was beginning to act depressed. He didn't go out to play with his friends as much as he used to. He even stopped watching TV. He seemed to spend most of his time alone in his room drawing pictures. (An assessment of Jason's pictures can be found in Appendix A.)

Holiday vacations came and went, and by the time Jason's battery of tests began, it was after the first of the year.

When the tests had been completed and evaluated, Barbara was called in for an "interpretive conference and PPT."

"What's a PPT?" she wondered.

"You'll find out when you get there," Mike answered.

When Barbara arrived for the "interpretive conference and PPT," she was overwhelmed to realize that this meeting included the school principal, the assistant principal, the nurse, the kindergarten teacher, the speech and hearing therapist, the school psychologist, and the reading specialist.

"What kind of overkill is this?" she wondered to herself. "All these big guns just for one little five-year-old boy?" She had trouble holding back a nervous giggle. But at the end of the session, she was in no mood to smile.

She was told that Jason had "high-average to superior IQ with significant scatter on verbal subtests. The emotional factors suggested anxiety and a negative self-image. The results, however, are not clear-cut." The discussion at this point covered several possibilities, ranging from neurological evaluation to psychiatric evaluation. Barbara's stomach began to churn. Everyone seemed to be talking to each other, not to her. In spite of the fact that the purpose of this meeting was to enlighten her, she did not feel enlightened. In fact, she felt more in the dark than ever, and she didn't understand half of the words these people were using.

Then the speech and hearing therapist brought up the unclear audiological evaluation done during Jason's preschool screening. "Does Jason get a lot of colds and congestion? And have you had his hearing re-evaluated?"

"Yes, he does get a lot of colds, but no, we haven't had his hearing re-evaluated. I didn't know we were supposed to."

The consensus of the meeting at that point was that Barbara should take Jason to an ear, nose, and throat specialist and have his hearing tested. But they made no recommendations as to whom she should consult.

Barbara called Dr. Brumley, who gave her the name of a specialist.

After examining Jason, the specialist called Mike and Barbara into his office. "Probably as a result of the colds and congestion Jason suffered when he was two, he has enlarged adenoids and fluid in his middle ear and a significant hearing loss."

Mike and Barbara looked at each other. No wonder Jason was having problems in school! He didn't come when he was called because he didn't *know* he was being called. He couldn't follow directions because he couldn't *hear* the directions. He didn't play well with other kids because he never quite understood everything they were saying. And in his frustration, he lashed out at everyone around him.

They were overwhelmed with relief. At last, they knew what was wrong! Now everything would be fine. "What do we do?"

"Jason needs surgery. We'll take out those adenoids, and we'll put small drainage tubes in each ear. That will help to drain the fluids into his throat, and it will keep his ears clear so he'll be able to hear well."

Surgery was scheduled for the following week, and it went off without a hitch.

When Jason went back to school, he showed immediate improvement in listening; however, some of his behavioral problems continued. Jason had learned to meet frustration with anger; he had to unlearn some of his patterns of behavior and establish new ones. The school initiated a small play-group guidance program, with Jason as one of the children in the group.

In June, Barbara went into the school for the year's last conference with the kindergarten teacher. Mrs. Berquist greeted her with a smile.

"I can't begin to tell you how much Jason has improved! He listens better, he's much more cooperative, he gets along better with the other kids, and his reading-readiness skills are almost up where they belong. By the end of next year, I think he'll have caught up with his peers and even surpassed some of them."

Barbara was pleased to hear that. And she was glad to be able to tell Mrs. Berquist that things had improved with Jason at home, too. But as she walked out to her car, she knew that, in spite of Jason's improvement, everything wasn't really "fine," as she had hoped when the problem was diagnosed. Jason might never again be the confident, outgoing, trusting person she and Mike had once enjoyed. He had spent more than two lost and lonely years enduring failure and frustration that were not his fault—and those years could never be recovered.

The story of Jason, Barbara, and Mike Evans is typical in several ways. Like most parents, when Mike and Barbara sensed a problem with their son, they searched for answers. They placed a great deal of trust in the professionals, who "ought to know," but they were never able to give the full story accurately and completely to these professionals, who ended up working on partial information. They relied on their pediatrician to tell them if anything was wrong with Jason. They looked for help and counsel from their parents and their neighbors, and they disagreed often over how the problem should be handled. In short, they didn't know what to do or who to turn to. They were floundering, and it was really a matter of luck and perseverence that they finally found out what the problem was and how to deal with it.

If the Evanses had been able to keep tabs on Jason's abilities and growth in some measured way, they might have been alerted sooner to the fact that Jason had a problem. Consistent observations and testing games, with recorded results, might have revealed that at about his third year, Jason underwent a *decline* in physical skills involving balance—a clue that can indicate inner-ear problems. His parents might have noted that Jason spoke more clearly at two and a half than he did at three and a half—or that he didn't feel as happy about himself at four as he had at three.

Armed with this specific information, Mike and Barbara might have been able to find the right specialists and get help faster. That's what we mean when we say that only systematic observation can clue you in to your child's progress and problems.

And when it comes to making systematic observations of a child's ongoing progress, which expert is in the best position to watch and test and compare this month to last month or last year? The one expert whose specialty is your child: you.

There's one other thing to be learned from Barbara Evans's struggle to pinpoint her son's problem: Professional sources—the schools and doctors in your community—are anxious to help, but they can't do it alone. It's a team effort, and you, the parents, are important members of the team. In fact, you're the team managers. It's up to you to stay on top of things and to coordinate team activities; to make sure that permission forms are sent and tests are scheduled and that the various team members each know what the other teammates are doing. Your involvement is crucial. Because if there's one thing you know from your years as a parent, it's this: Raising a child is not a spectator sport.

□2□

Professional Testing and Human Abilities

When you talk to professionals in child development—and by professionals we mean anyone from the teacher through the school psychologist to the neurologist or the psychiatrist—you will find that most of them have one thing in common: even the most well-meaning and understanding of them tends to use a language that an ordinary person finds befuddling. They can't help it. For them, it's a kind of shorthand. They spend so much time talking about "planning and placement teams" and "Individual Educational Plans"—it's just easier for them to say "PPT" and "IEP." When they toss off references to "standardized" tests or "Stanford-Binet," *they* know what they're talking about, and it's easy for them to forget that you don't. How is a parent to understand that a "wisk" and a "rat" are kinds of ability tests?

That's why we're going to spend some time here talking about human abilities and the tests the professionals administer to evaluate these abilities. That way, you'll know, when the time comes, what the professionals are talking about; you'll be able to talk back to them. You'll be able to create a dialogue out of a situation that could have been a monologue delivered in a foreign language.

HUMAN ABILITIES

Early sailors were hampered in their exploration of the world by the fact that they couldn't sail out of sight of the land. If they did, they got

25

lost. When they mapped the land, they could put up markers to show where they'd been and how far they'd come. But on the high seas, this was obviously impossible. It does no good, of course, to put an X on the side of the boat to mark your position!

When mariners developed the ability to navigate in terms of distance, speed, and time, they could sail anywhere in the world and still figure out where they were. They had learned to measure progress and position based on the passage of time.

It's much the same when you try to measure human abilities. If you try to gauge Genevieve's motor or verbal skills only by looking at where she is right now, you're just marking an X on the side of the boat. Abilities can best be measured in terms of growth—and this means that systematic observations and measurements are required over time.

Human abilities begin to develop in infancy. Genevieve spends her first days and months learning how to taste and smell her food, hear the sounds of her world, find out what things feel like and what things look like. These are the *sensory* abilities. As she grows older, she begins to organize what she has learned about tasting, smelling, hearing, feeling, and seeing into useful patterns of knowledge. She finds out that things that look like bread have a particular taste and smell. She sees that the things she drops from her high-chair tray fall down, and that her plate won't fit into her cup. She learns that the kitty feels soft and fluffy, and that she doesn't ever want to touch the stove burner again. These are the *perceptual* abilities.

Soon she realizes that when she hears Mommy's voice, it means Mommy is nearby. This is a *symbolic* ability. Later she can refine that understanding even more. If she is hungry and she hears Mommy nearby, that's good; it means she can have lunch soon. If she's sneaking a forbidden cookie and she hears Mommy's voice nearby, that's *not* good: it probably means a swat on the bottom! This is a very simple form of *conceptual* ability.

When Genevieve reaches school age, she will apply the skills she has learned to special activities involving codes and symbols and concepts. She will learn that, just as Mommy's voice symbolized Mommy, the letter

A symbolizes a certain sound. She'll learn "reading, 'riting, and 'rithmetic." She will build skill upon skill, adding to what she already knows about learning, until she becomes a chef or a physicist or a journalist or a florist or a houseperson or a teacher—whatever occupation fits her special skills and abilities and gives her satisfaction.

There was a time when people didn't understand that human abilities are built skill by skill. Many primitive tribes thought it was a matter of magic, of having the right totem. If your totem was the cat, you would have sharp eyes and great cunning. If your totem was the bear, you would have strength. If you didn't have a good totem, too bad for you.

Psychology has helped to lead us away from magic and mythology and into a world where we can observe, attempt to measure, and try to understand how people learn and what can be done to help them learn better. We still don't know everything. We're still making guesses, as the primitive tribes did. But they're based on measures, not on myths.

So let's take a look at some of these measures.

PRINCIPLES OF PSYCHOLOGICAL TESTING

What Is a Psychological Test?

Basically, a psychological test is an objective and standardized measure of a sample of behavior.

The term *objective* refers to the fact that test administration, scoring, and interpretation of scores are all accomplished in an unbiased manner, that is, independent of the subjective judgment of the examiner. In other words, the examiner does not let his or her own wishes, beliefs, and hopes affect the results.

The term *standardized* means that the tests are administered, scored, and interpreted through uniform procedures that are specified in the test manual. In other words, the tests are always given the same way, no matter who does it or whether it's done in Bangor, Maine, or Bangkok, Thailand.

Finally, *sample of behavior* refers to behavior that is representative of the individual's usual behavior outside of the test situation. In other words, it is assumed that the way the child performs on the test is typical of that child's usual performance level.

What Is a Psychoeducational Assessment?

Psychoeducational assessment refers to the administration of both psychological and educational tests and the use of both psychological and educational theories in an attempt to understand the child's learning style and problems and to determine what can be done to help correct the situation.

How Good Is a Test?

You won't be surprised to learn that there are myriad difficulties involved in attempting to measure anything as variable as human behavior. (People do seem to be so complex!) We won't try to explain all these difficulties, but it may be helpful for you to know about two terms used to discuss how good a test is: reliability and validity.

Reliability refers to the consistency and stability of measurement by the test. In other words, how consistent are the scores obtained by the same person when retested with either the same test or an equivalent form of the test?

Validity refers to the extent to which the test actually measures what it sets out to measure.

To make this a bit clearer, let's imagine measuring a box with a ruler made of stretchable elastic. The first time you measure the height, you might come up with a figure of eleven inches. But the next time you measure, if you stretch the ruler more, you might come up with a height of eight inches for the same box. And if a friend tries to measure the same box with the same ruler, the measurement might be nine inches. So which is it—Eleven? Eight? Nine? Clearly a rubber ruler is not reliable.

Now suppose you get a metal ruler. Not much stretch there. Each time you measure, and each time your friend measures, you get the same number—let's say it's nine inches. Now we have a reliable measuring device for size—a metal ruler.

Suppose, however, that your friend wants to know how heavy the box is. You take your metal ruler and measure each side: nine inches high, six inches wide, and four inches across. If you tell your friend the box is nine by six by four inches heavy, he still won't know how much the box weighs. Measuring weight with a ruler is not valid.

What Is the Difference Between Norm-Referenced Tests and Criterion-Referenced Tests?

Norm-referenced tests are those in which a child's score is determined by comparing that child's performance to a sample of other children who have performed the same tasks. For norm-referenced tests, a number line is created by testing many kids and arranging the results from best to worst. The scores in the middle of the line are called the *norm*.

Criterion-referenced tests are those in which a child's score is determined by how many kinds of tasks the child can do, without comparison to the performance of other children.

For instance, if Genevieve goes out for Little League baseball and the coach says that, to make the team, she has to get two hits out of three pitches and catch three out of five ground balls and throw the distance from first base to home, that is a criterion-referenced test. Can she do certain tasks at the level expected?

Now, if the coach had been keeping records over the years and had found that 50 percent of the kids who tried out could hit one out of three pitches, but that only 20 percent could hit two out of three, and that 5 percent hit three out of three, he would have the basis for a kind of norm-referenced test based on his sample of ballplayers. He could compare each child trying out to other kids who had tried out, and he could rate Genevieve not only in terms of whether she could meet the criterion he set but also in terms of how she compared to other kids.

You may note that a criterion-referenced test, if it is to make sense, must set a realistic level of expectation. No Little League coach could require that his eight-year-olds throw the ball from center field to home or bat a thousand—not if he expects to field nine players that year!

We should note that the tests and observations in this book are criterion-referenced. You'll be seeing if your child can or cannot do each task; you won't actually be getting a score that makes a specific comparison to the level of other children. However, to ensure that the items on the tests and in the games are realistic, they have been based on the norms of reference that have been developed by many childhood researchers, as well as on our own experience with children. You will be getting criterion-based measures. The items have not been presented to a sample of children in order to obtain a scoring system. Our criterion is that most kids can do these tasks, and you can check to see whether your child can do them, too.

To review, then: A norm-referenced test reports where each child stands on the test in relation to the placement of children in the norm group. In contrast, criterion-referenced tests compare each child's level of mastery to the scope of knowledge or skill that the test has been designed to cover. Since criterion-referenced tests compare the child's performance against mastery of a skill, they generally have more relevance for instructional purposes.

The results of norm-referenced tests are presented in a variety of ways, including percentile ranks, stanines, and grade or age equivalents. What do these mean?

Percentile rank indicates that a percentage of students in a norm group at a given grade or age scored at or below a given raw score. (The raw score is the number of items the child answered correctly.) For example, if Genevieve is assigned a percentile rank of 85 on a norm-referenced math test, this means that 85 percent of the students in the norm group at her age or grade scored as well as or lower than she did. This translation of Genevieve's raw score gives an indication of her standing in comparison with others in the same age or grade group.

CAUTION: A characteristic of percentile ranks is that toward the middle of the scale, an increase of only a few raw score points tends to result in a marked increase in percentile rank. This means that John may score 76 right answers and be in the sixty-fifth percentile, while Julie scores 78 right and is in the seventy-second percentile—a big leap in percentile caused by just two more correct answers on the test. On the other hand, the same increase in raw score points at either the high or low end of the scale (below the tenth percentile and above the ninetieth) results in only a small increase in percentile rank points.

Stanines (pronounced "Stay-nines") are scores in a scale ranging from 1 to 9, with 5 representing the average performance of the norm group. This scoring system is often used in school-administered evaluations.

Grade equivalents provide a score that indicates how the student's performance compares with that of others at the same grade level. The score represents both the school grade and the month of the school year. For example, 1.3 means first grade, third month of school (November).

Although grade equivalents have long been popular ways to report the test performance of school-age children, they are losing their popularity because of some significant drawbacks. The most important of these is the frequent misinterpretation of what the scores mean. For example, if Genevieve, in second grade, gets 3.7 on a science test, some people think that this means she should be instructed with third-grade science materials—textbooks and so on. Not so. What this score really means is that the student is better than the average second-grader at second-grade work; it does not mean that she can do third-grade work. The same caution applies to age equivalent scores.

What's the Difference Between a Screening and an Assessment?

Screening. The purpose of developmental screening is to find out whether a child should be more closely evaluated to determine if she needs special services. A child's performance in the area of motor, social-personal, language, and cognitive behaviors is generally observed in a play setting. These screenings generally include physical exams, hearing and visual-acuity tests, and speech/language surveys. Some nursery schools conduct screenings, and many public schools routinely screen youngsters before they enter kindergarten. These are not entrance exams, which a child might "flunk," but a first-time measure against which growth can be judged.

A note here is required, however, since it is sometimes the case that a child who has difficulty in many of the skills checked in the preschool screening may be identified as a child who is "not ready for kindergarten." In this case, the parents are advised to let the child grow for an extra year before enrolling him or her in kindergarten. Many children simply need a bit more time to reach the level required for school success. For instance, Genevieve may be "ready" for everything she might encounter in kindergarten, but then she may, after that year, be "unready" for the greater demands of first grade. Rather than having her repeat kindergarten, educators may advise holding her out of kindergarten for a year. This decision is often made for children whose birthday falls close to the cut-off age for admission; they would be six or more months younger than their classmates.

It is also true that more boys than girls seem to lack the language, motor, and attention or social skills needed to begin school. These boys are sometimes advised to stay out the extra year.

If in a screening of some sort your child is identified as "immature,"or not ready for kindergarten, ask to have those expressions defined in terms of specific areas of difficulty. Then, although there is generally no cause for alarm, determine what further evaluation may be appropriate, and follow through with professional assistance if you feel the need. Ninety to 95 percent of these cases require no specific help or remediation, but the 5 percent who do can profit from getting that help early.

Full Assessment. This is a complete and exhaustive review of the child's skills, strengths, and deficits. It may include such procedures as IQ testing, personality testing, and perceptual/motor testing. During a full assessment, an attempt is made to determine if a problem exists. If one does, information regarding the child's strengths and weaknesses is accumulated in order to develop an individualized program for that child.

What Do IQ Tests Determine?

The first IQ test was not intended to pinpoint intelligence. It was part of the French government's attempt to discover which children were retarded and therefore needed special schooling. Alfred Binet, a French psychologist with an interest in abnormal persons, was asked to design a test that would identify students who were below normal in intelligence. In the process, Binet and his associate, Theodore Simon, discovered that there was a relationship between a child's age and the tasks the child could perform. Children who were later than average in developing the ability for basic tasks were predictably slower in their overall development than those children who performed the tasks at a younger age. In other words, they were behind their fellow students: retarded.

How did Binet and Simon determine what was "average"? They simply determined that what most children could do was, by definition, average. If most children can draw a simple house, solve an eight-piece puzzle, and repeat their address by the age of six, then that becomes the norm to compare all children to. Those who can perform these tasks at an earlier age are given higher scores; those who can't perform the tasks until they are older than six are given lower scores. Of course there are many more tasks involved than the three we have mentioned—but you get the basic idea. Binet tested thousands of children, found out *from them* what was normal, and developed a scoring system based upon higher scores for earlier performance and lower scores for later performance.

Here we have the basis for a problem that has continued to plague testing in general. We tend to think that *normal* is synonymous with *all right*—and that's not true. Genevieve can be "not normal"—that is, her scores may fall outside the area where most kids' scores lie—and she can still be perfectly all right. (That's partly what this book is all about—to correct the mistaken idea that it's best to be normal and bad to be different.)

The IQ test has been refined and readjusted often since Binet and Simon first developed their version at the turn of the century. Today we know that the IQ test is not nearly as precise an instrument as people used to believe. And here we come to another very big problem with IQ tests: they attempt to measure human abilities—which can't be directly observed. You can't dissect Genevieve to see what her abilities are. You can only watch what she does, observe the skills and behaviors she exhibits, and then make guesses. Nobody can ever know for sure what a child's ability is, because we can never see the ability itself. (This is what scientists call the "black box" phenomenon.) It's not like measuring a pulse rate. The doctor who takes Genevieve's pulse and discovers it's 93 knows exactly how fast her heart is beating. The doctor is measuring something concrete and tangible. But a psychologist who "measures" Genevieve's ability is only determining what she *shows* she can do. It is not necessarily a measure of Genevieve's real ability.

It's important for you to know that IQ tests aren't real measures of anything absolute and tangible. They are simply ways of making guesses about abilities. Educated guesses, of course, but still only guesses.

Another thing it's important to remember is that an IQ is a *score* derived from a particular test that is labeled an intelligence test. It is a way of expressing the results on a particular test. If you consider only the score without understanding how that score was reached, you are not only neglecting important information about the child, but you are also likely to draw inappropriate conclusions about the child.

Look at it this way: When the Little League Tigers play the Bears, and the Tigers lose 5 to 3, does that make the Tigers a "3"? Are the Bears a "5"? Of course not. The Tigers are a team of hardworking, go-for-it kids who played their hearts out. Their fielding was terrific—they even had a great double play. The Bears are another team of hardworking, go-for-it kids, who happened not to make any major mistakes. Last month when the same two teams played, the Tigers won 6–3. Were the Tigers a "6" and the Bears a "3"? No way! Those scores were just a convenient way to keep track of and to record what happened on those two days. But if you look at just one score, you might think that the Tigers were "losers."

A baseball team is not its score. And neither is a child.

So What Is an Intelligence Test?

Intelligence tests are measures of scholastic aptitude. Test scores reflect Genevieve's prior achievement, and they predict her future performance. By identifying her capabilities, we are better able to anticipate the child's future needs—particularly if specific help may be necessary.

Can Your IQ Change?

Historically, there have been three schools of thought on this matter.

The first maintains that your intellectual potential is genetically determined: if your parents and grandparents are intelligent, you probably will be, too.

The second emphasizes environmental factors in the formation of intelligence. Tarzan lovers may be disappointed to hear that if you are raised from infancy by a tribe of apes, you will *not* be able to teach yourself to read and write English. It is unlikely that you will perform well on a standard IQ test. On the other hand, you will not necessarily have the IQ of an ape.

The third and possibly most widely held theory is that a child is born with a range of intellectual capacity; that this range varies among individuals; and that environmental experiences play an important role in determining where each child will function within this range. (If you inherit average intelligence but are denied schooling, your IQ will probably be lower than it might have been if you'd had ample opportunities for schooling with inspiring teachers.) In other words, the innate potential for intellectual development can be affected by a variety of environmental variables. Based on this third school of thought, many students of human behavior have concluded that a person's IQ can and does change as the person develops and changes.

Is It Possible to Determine the Intellectual Potential
of Infants and Very Young Children?

Infant intelligence tests grew out of attempts to relate the early development of motor, sensory, language, and social skills to intellectual behavior. However, with children under the age of three, standardized tests have proven to be relatively poor predictors of future intellectual functioning. Therefore, standardized tests for very young children are generally used only to assess a child's current status rather than to predict future ability levels. So if your three-year-old scores high, it's too early to assume that you're raising a genius; and if she scores low, it's also wrong to assume that you have a long-term problem.

What About Testing Minorities?

In the 1960s, a great deal of public attention was devoted to the fact that the norms for most IQ tests were weighted heavily in favor of some groups and against certain minorities.

Today, efforts are being made to create tests that are not culturally biased by sex, race, creed, or color. The interpretation of tests by professionals these days is very carefully considered, taking into account the child's background. We have, we hope, moved beyond the biases and misuses of the past, so parents need not be as concerned about this as before. However, it is a good idea to be aware that cultural differences may be reflected in test results. If your child's background is such that he or she might not be expected to understand some things that are a basic part of the typical American child's experience, you should notify your child's examiner. The examiner will then take these factors into consideration when compiling test results.

Appendix B contains a list of the tests frequently used in working with young children.

What Is "Child Find"?

Since the 1970s, the United States has been committed to a program of actively locating children who are at risk of being handicapped by any area of difficulty in their development. By law, all states now have facilities for locating these children. (The principle is much the same as the early efforts in France to locate retarded children, though on a much broader scale, and with the power of the media to promote public awareness.) Professionals—pediatricians, visiting nurses, teachers—are instructed to notify Child Find if they believe a child is at risk of becoming handicapped. But for very young children who are at home most of the time, the parents are most likely to be the ones who suspect a problem. Parents who suspect that their child may need special education can get in touch with the nearest Child Find service, and they will be directed to the proper agencies for the appropriate help. Call your local board of education, even if your child is a preschooler, if you want to get in touch with Child Find.

How to Observe and Record Your Child's Progress

WHEN TO OBSERVE

There is a time to test and a time to refrain from testing, and knowing which is which can have a marked effect on your child's performance.

If you choose your time well, the responses you get on the games in this book will be pretty good indicators of ability; if you choose the wrong moment, your child's responses and scores may suffer.

It won't pay to pull Jeffrey away from some activity he is enjoying—even if it's only a Road Runner or Bugs Bunny cartoon—to "play the games" in this book. He'll only be thinking about how Road Runner can give Wile E. Coyote the slip, or wondering why mothers always interrupt just at the best part. You won't get his full attention, and you'll almost certainly get an unrealistically low score.

Pick a time when Jeffrey is at loose ends. When he comes into the kitchen saying, "Mommy, I don't have anything to do," or, "Dad, I don't have anyone to play with," that's the perfect time to play one or two of the games.

Or if you make it a practice to set aside some time each day to spend alone with your child, that might be just the right moment to play one of the games in this book.

HOW LONG SHOULD A SESSION LAST?

A child of three to five years may have a short attention span. There's no way you can stretch it out; you just have to accept it and work with it. Play one of the games. If Jeffrey is still alert and interested, you might want to try another, but two is probably as many as you'll want to do at one sitting. In any event, don't attempt to go through the whole book in a day, or even in a week. Take it easy; enjoy the games; make them last.

If your child loses interest in the middle of a game, don't press him to do "just two more questions, and then we're all done." Stop immediately when the fun goes out of the game. Next time you try it—in a few days or weeks—he may want to finish it. Or he may not. This, too, is part of knowing who your child is.

When you've finished the game or games, play something else with Jeffrey. Play catch; play house; talk for a few minutes. Not only will this help you both to wind down, it will make the games in the book seem like an everyday part of life, not like something of special importance.

Be open, but don't suggest to Jeffrey that what you are doing is terribly special or important. "I found this book that has a lot of games in it that we can play" is one approach. Or "Here's a book that will help us measure some of the things you do. Let's try some of the games."

Keep the test situation casual. If equipment is called for, don't have it ready ahead of time like a stage set in a play. Instead, let Jeffrey help gather the materials: "The book says we need scissors and a pencil. Do you know where your scissors are?"

Sit on the floor or at a table, wherever you both are accustomed to sitting together and are comfortable.

It is not necessary—or advisable—to hide the fact that you are writing down his answers. In fact, if you try to be secretive, you may only make your youngster suspect that something is being put over on him. This can create resistance to the game or distract him. Instead, be relaxed and completely open. Most children are familiar with games that require some form of scorekeeping, and that's basically what you are doing— keeping score. Just let the child know you are marking the ones he can do already, and that the others you'll do when he's older. Our scoring system allows you to mark only successes and leave the others blank.

Ask each question clearly, making sure you have your youngster's attention. Allow a reasonable amount of time for the answer. If you think he may not have heard or understood, repeat it once—but don't repeat it more often than that. If the child answers incorrectly, move on. Never repeat the question at that point, since even young children have learned to change an answer if asked again. They will often even change a correct answer.

SUPPORT VS. EVALUATION

It's natural for a parent to respond with enthusiasm when a youngster does something well or correctly, or to urge a different or better answer if he has done it "wrong." In a testing situation, however, you'll want to control these responses to avoid influencing the child's performance. This doesn't mean that you should avoid making any responses. It does mean that you should try to develop the kind of responses that will show Jeffrey that you are enjoying the game, that you are supporting him but not evaluating him.

An evaluative response judges the child's work—and the child. And although there may be times and places when evaluation and judgment are necessary, the middle of a test is not one of them. The child becomes aware of being judged. Jeffrey may try too hard, or he may give up, feeling that it's not worth the effort. Either reaction, of course, will make a difference in his scores.

A supportive response encourages the child without offering condemnation—or unrealistic praise. And children do know when they are being overpraised.

Take five-year-old Susan, for instance. She shows her mother a page she has colored in a coloring book. "Susan, that's wonderful! That's the best coloring job I've ever seen!" her well-intentioned mother rhapsodizes. But Susan knows better. She can see places where she has gone out of the lines, and she doesn't really like the way she colored the dress pink and orange. "Mommy is just saying it's good because she's my mom," Susan decides. So the next picture she shows her mother has even more places where she went outside the lines, and the boy's hair is purple—which any baby knows is silly! But Mommy's response is still full of praise. Susan is upset. Doesn't her mother know that she can do better than that?

So picture number three is good and sloppy. And now Susan gets more than she bargained for. "Susan, you know you can do better than that! That's no good! It's just a mess!" In spite of the fact that Susan wanted her mother to realize that this was not a good job, she is devastated. Her mother still doesn't seem to understand what kind of work Susan really does, and her angry overreaction to the picture hurts.

What would have helped Susan and her mother would have been some middle-ground responses that reflected appreciation without making any judgments, pro or con. "You worked hard on this picture." "A pink blouse with an orange skirt—look at that!" "I see purple hair! I see you smiling about your picture!" Supportive, interested comments such as these would show Susan that her mother is paying attention, that she knows what Susan's usual style is.

Non-evaluative comments are sometimes hard to come up with on the spur of the moment, especially when you have been used to offering praise or criticism. It doesn't hurt to have a repertoire of such comments that you can bring out in any situation—particularly when you are playing the games in this book: "Fine!" "Good!" "That was fun." "I'm enjoying this, aren't you?" "Good going!" Even "Super!" can be positive and supportive without being evaluative if you don't attach it to anything: not "Super answer!" or "Super kid!"—just "Super!"

Use these responses and others like them to recognize not only good work or good answers but good *effort*, willingness to respond; recognize also the child's enjoyment or effort or persistence.

It may also be helpful to recognize evaluative answers, so that you can avoid using them whenever possible. "Yes," "no," "right," and "wrong" are all evaluative. "You can do better." "That's the best you've done yet." "Try harder." "Listen!" "Pay attention." "I know you could do this if you worked at it." All of these remarks imply evaluation and/or criticism.

Supportive, non-evaluative comments are useful tools for communicating in all areas of a child's life; they are especially appropriate in a testing situation because they indicate to Jeffrey that you are paying attention, that his response has reached you, that there is communication between you. But they do not cause him to think, "Hey, this is easy— I can do it without half trying!" or "Boy, this is too hard for me. I can't get it right no matter what I do." Either of these attitudes would probably have an effect on his performance.

This is not to say that you will not be making judgments. That would be impossible. Furthermore, it is necessary for you to make judgments to yourself if you are to help Jeffrey achieve his full potential. You want to recognize those areas in which he performs above or below the average, and of course to make this determination, some evaluation is necessary. However, it is not necessary to pass these evaluations on to the child.

What if Jeffrey asks, "How did I do on the game? Did I win?" You can say "You did fine" or "You seem to be having fun" or "We had fun, didn't we?" You can say this whether he answered every question correctly or incorrectly. You can say that there are many things he can do already. And you can emphasize that the next time you play the game, he or she will be older and will probably be able to do even harder ones.

You can tell your preschooler that "this is a book all about you." Explain that you're going to find out all the things he can do, and that every time you do these activities, he will be able to do more and more of them, so you'll both be able to see how he grows. By emphasizing the growing, you build up confidence that even if Jeffrey lacks the skill now, he or she will gain it eventually.

When you have played the games and done the activities, and when Jeffrey has done the drawings, you'll have a permanent record of your child's path of development. It may be that someday this record will come in handy. If Jeffrey's path seems to wander—if he begins to have trouble with reading, or if you become concerned about him in any way, so that it seems wise to consult professional counselors—the information in this book may be very helpful. But it's much more likely that your child will grow and develop smoothly, with no more detours than any other growing child takes along the path. In that case, having a record of your child's achievements is just plain fun.

It won't surprise you to learn that if Jeffrey is under stress, he won't do as well on any kind of game or test. But you might not have realized that *your* stress can affect your child's work, too.

If you're going through a stressful period, Jeffrey will feel your tension and will react to it—perhaps by resisting everything you ask or by trying too hard in an effort to please you. So if you've been having a tough time over the past few weeks, it might be better to put off playing and scoring the games in this book.

Here's a test for *you* to take to check your stress level. If, in evaluating the events of the past six months or so, you have checked off one or more high-stress items, or several moderate-stress items, you might want to wait awhile before playing the testing games with your child.

STRESS TEST FOR PARENTS

Life Event	*(Check those that apply.)*	
1. Death of spouse, child, close family member	____	
2. Divorce or separation	____	
3. Unwanted pregnancy	____	
4. Strong feelings of anxiety or depression	____	
5. Alcoholism in family	____	
6. Serious marital discord	____	*High-stress events*
7. Personal injury or illness	____	
8. Remarriage	____	
9. Loss of job or significant portion of income	____	
10. Serious financial problems, such as foreclosure	____	
11. Problems with older child(ren)	____	

Life Event	*(Check those that apply.)*	
12. Being victim of a crime	_____	
13. Significant illness of family member	_____	
14. Wanted pregnancy	_____	
15. You and/or spouse return to school	_____	
16. Sex difficulties	_____	
17. Family discord centered on children	_____	
18. Birth or adoption of a child	_____	
19. Child has accident requiring hospitalization	_____	*Moderate-stress events*
20. Change in financial state	_____	
21. Death of a close friend	_____	
22. Change of jobs	_____	
23. Child having serious difficulties in school	_____	
24. New or additional mortgage	_____	
25. Difficulties in toilet training a child	_____	
26. Son or daughter leaving home	_____	
27. Trouble with in-laws	_____	
28. Outstanding personal achievement	_____	
29. Change in living conditions or work	_____	*Lower-stress events*
30. Moving	_____	
31. Change in sleeping or eating habits	_____	
32. Minor violations of the law	_____	
33. Vacation, Christmas, or holidays	_____	

No life is absolutely free of stress, nor would we wish it to be. You will have observed that some of the items on our list, such as a wanted pregnancy or the birth or adoption of a child, may in fact be delightful, even though they do cause some disturbance in the parents' lives!

If you are under a lot of stress, or are besieged by many other stress items, your own stress may cause your child to perform in a way that is not typical, distorting his or her scores. You may want to hold off on playing the games and tests in this book until your own life is a little more serene.

GENERAL SCORING INSTRUCTIONS

Okay, now that you know in general how to observe and record your child's development, how do you use this book to help you observe and record?

Easily. At the end of each skill chapter (the chapters discussing particular abilities), you'll find a set of games and observations with a system for recording and scoring your child's responses to each item. In general, this scoring will allow you to indicate if a skill is present or just emerging, or not there yet. Some skills are expected by a certain age; some are not. The scoring helps you sort out which is which. By scoring now, and again in the future, you will be able to see what is really important: progress or lack of progress.

After each question, you will see a scoring place for age levels three and a half, four and a half, and five and a half. At each age level, you will find either a dotted box or a solid box. The dotted box indicates that this skill may be emerging at this age but is not expected to be solidly achieved by most children. In other words, at this age level, most children do not know the correct response to that question. The solid box, however, means that, at this age level, most children *can* demonstrate the correct response.

We have indicated that the games and tests should be played approximately at three and a half, four and a half, and five and a half years of age. We have designated these ages for the activities we selected because at these ages most children have these skills well in hand. But you don't have to count the days until your child is exactly three years and six months old. Any time within two or three months before or after our selected ages will be fine.

When a dotted box appears: If the child does give a good, correct response, put a *plus* in the dotted box. (A correct answer is more than is expected for most children on this item, so a correct response means the child is ahead of expectations.)

If your child does not respond, or gives a minimal or inaccurate response, draw a line completely through the box. (The line means that you have tried the item.) Since this is an emerging skill, his response is acceptable but is not scored, because a fully correct response is not expected.

When a solid box appears: If your child gives a generally correct response, put a check in the solid box, indicating an acceptable response for that age. For some items, a specific level of accomplishment will be stated in parentheses below the response line. When a level is specifically stated, score a check if the child is *at* this level; score a plus if the response is *above* this level. If your child does not respond correctly, leave the box blank. This indicates that your child did not respond correctly to an item most children at that age can respond to.

Remember: A check indicates the expected level of performance. A plus indicates a better-than-average response. A blank solid box indicates a lower-than-average response. *Dotted* boxes with lines drawn through them indicate that these items, although not correctly answered, are to be disregarded. Many children have not yet achieved these skills at the given age.

This scoring system may seem complicated until you begin to use it. At that point you will find that it is quite easy: All you have to do is put checks or pluses in the boxes. We have provided some sample scoring possibilities below.

Note: Not all the games and activities are scored. Some are samples for you to have and keep, like the locks of baby hair from the first haircut, just for the joy of remembering and seeing Jeffrey's progress. If now or in the future you begin to be concerned about your child, you may share the drawings and tests with professionals; the specialists may find these materials helpful in getting a clear idea of his growth over time.

BUILDING A TOWER

Instructions: For this activity, you'll need twelve square alphabet blocks. Place a block in front of your child. Start stacking them one on top of another until it is three blocks high. Then say, "You finish the tower. See how high you can go."

	Age		
	3½	4½	5½

1. Child stacks five blocks.   ⊞   ☐   ☐

   (Jeffrey, at 3½, stacks five blocks. Since the dotted box indicates that he is not expected to perform this task, his answer is above average. Score a plus.)

2. Child stacks eight blocks.   ⬚   ☑   ☐

   (Jeffrey, at 4½, stacks eight blocks—just the amount indicated above. Score a check. If he had stacked more than eight, he would have scored a plus.)

3. Child stacks twelve blocks.   ⬚   ⬚   ☐
   (Jeffrey, at 5½, stacks ten blocks—below the average response. Leave the box blank.)

Where no criterion is stated, you may use your judgment to determine whether the response is correct. If you are especially impressed with the quality of your child's response, put a plus in the box.

WHAT DO THEY DO?

	Age		
	3½	4½	5½

1. What does a doctor do?

3½	*"I don't know."*	⊡		

(Place a line through box for this incorrect answer. If there is a dotted box, most children are not expected to answer correctly at that age, and the line through the box simply means that you are disregarding this item.)

4½	*"Help dollies."*		☐	

(Leave blank if incorrect. The solid box indicates that most children will get this item right at this age.)

5½	*"Give medicine and treat sickness."*			☑

(For this correct answer, place a check in the box. This indicates that this item has been answered correctly, as it is by most children at this age.)

2. What is a refrigerator for?

3½	*"Keep food in."*	⊞		

(If there is a dotted box, and the answer is correct, score a plus. This means that because most children are not expected to get this item at this age, your child's response is above average.)

		Age	
	3½	4½	5½

4½	*"So food keeps good."*		☑	

(A check in the solid box means your child answered correctly an item answered correctly by most children at that age.)

5½	*"Keep food from spoiling."*			☑

(A check in the solid box means your child answered correctly an item answered correctly by most children.)

A LOOK AT YOUR RESULTS

After you've done all the activities in one section and checked the items according to your child's response, you'll be able to get an idea of your child's level in that area. Have you put checks in most of the solid boxes in that section? Then your child is doing what is expected of most children at that age.

Are there a number of blank boxes? You may find one or two blanks even for children who are generally at the same level as or ahead of their age group. Children are individuals—not everyone can do equally well on every activity. So one or two blank boxes should not be cause for concern. (A dotted box with a line through it is simply to be disregarded.) However, if there are more than two or three blank boxes in any section, this should alert you to the fact that your child may not be able to perform tasks that most children of that age can do. If this is the case, you will want to turn to our follow-up suggestions at the end of each skills section for ways in which you can help your child develop these abilities. This section in each chapter will also provide more information about possible professional help in each area.

Do you see a lot of pluses in the boxes? This indicates that your child is performing ahead of the expected level in this area. Again, you will find our suggestions for encouraging your child in the skills section at the end of each chapter.

Note: The items we have selected represent skills and abilities most three- to five-year-old children can handle. The three-year-old who can do things that are expected only of four- or five-year-olds will show herself to be ahead of her age level. However, because we have not included items that are expected of seven- or eight-year-olds, the five-year-old who is well ahead of his age level and capable of handling tasks expected of seven-year-olds will not have a chance to demonstrate those advanced abilities. In other words, this book can tell you clearly if your three-year-old is performing ahead of his level—but not as clearly if your five-and-a-half-year-old is, since he will find fewer items in a group of tests that are of an advanced nature for a five-and-a-half-year-old child. (This is called the *ceiling effect,* and it occurs in most testing.)

□4□

The Child from Three to Five

S uppose you tried to analyze a playroomful of three-year-olds to see if you could come up with some concept of "The Average Three-Year-Old." You might discover that:

- 30 percent of all shoelaces are trailing;
- 14 percent of all noses are dripping;
- 11 percent of all pants are sagging;
- 90 percent of all barrettes are lost;
- 35 percent of all flies are unzipped.

Beyond that, there would be so many differences among the children, it might seem that no meaningful definition of "The Average Three-Year-Old" would be possible.

But this doesn't mean that there are absolutely no guidelines for "threeness," "fourness," or "fiveness." Students of child behavior over the decades have found that there are some basic skills and characteristics that are typical of the majority of children at given ages. Taken with the proper grain of salt (there is *no such thing* as a typical three-year-old, and let's never forget that!), these skills and characteristics can help you to track your child's progress along that path from threeness to fiveness.

During the years between three and five, your Joanie will make some important changes—physical changes, of course. The physical changes are easy to recognize. You probably have one sacred doorway in your home that can never be washed because that's where you keep track of your child's growth, marking off the extra inches on each birthday and marveling at the huge space between this year's line and last year's. But there are also some changes in personality and in skills that come on gradually—in fact, they tend to sneak up on you. When the first day of kindergarten comes, you'll walk your daughter to the bus stop, wondering, Where did that potbellied, chubby-cheeked toddler go—the one who starting crying the minute she saw the babysitter coming up the walk, and whose pictures of Mommy resembled nothing so much as a lollipop? Somehow, she has changed into a long, skinny (How can she be skinny and still have dimples in her elbows?!), self-possessed young lady who can already write her own name, and who hops on the school bus without even remembering to wave good-bye.

How does a child get from three to five? It's a matter of gradual growth and development—of passages, you might say, from one stage to another. And although all children pass through all the stages, there's no universal timetable. It's not like a European cruise, where you know if it's Thursday, this must be Denmark. You can't point at a child and say, "He's tying his own shoes—he must be five years and two months."

But although there is no *universal* timetable, each child does have his or her *individual* timetable—and most individual timetables for growth and development follow a schedule of skills. In other words, you probably can point at that child who is tying his own shoes and say, "He already knows how to put on his pants and zip them by himself." Because most children, in reaching the shoe-tying stage, first pass through the pants-zipping stage. They master the simpler manipulative skill first and build on it to achieve the more difficult manipulative skills.

GROWTH AND DEVELOPMENT

We've used the words *growth* and *development* almost as if they were one and the same thing. This isn't true. There is an important difference between these two concepts.

Growth is mostly a matter of size and shape—and it's mostly prede-

HEIGHT-WEIGHT CHARTS FOR CHILDREN

Use the charts* on these pages to chart your child's weight and height. Take all measurements with the child in underwear, without shoes. To record measurements, find the child's age on the horizontal scale. Then follow a vertical line from that point

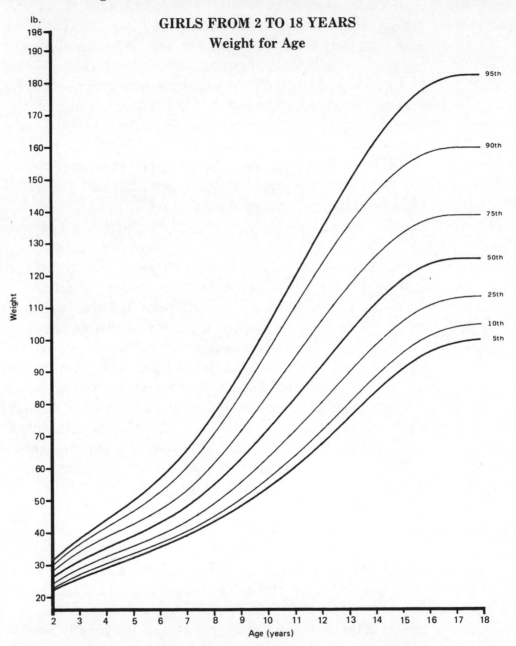

GIRLS FROM 2 TO 18 YEARS
Weight for Age

*Sources: Department of Health and Human Services; Public Health Service Health Resources Administration; National Center for Health Statistics; Center for Disease Control.

to the horizontal line indicating the child's height or weight, and mark the spot where the lines cross. This will tell you your child's rank in a group of 100. If he or she is at the ninety-fifth-percentile line, only 5 among 100 children of corresponding age and sex are heavier or taller.

Continue to use the same chart to record your child's growth over the years.

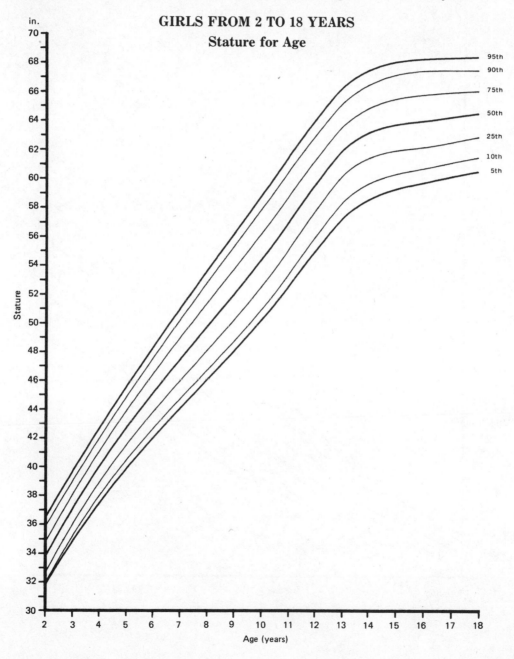

GIRLS FROM 2 TO 18 YEARS

Stature for Age

BOYS FROM 2 TO 18 YEARS
Weight for Age

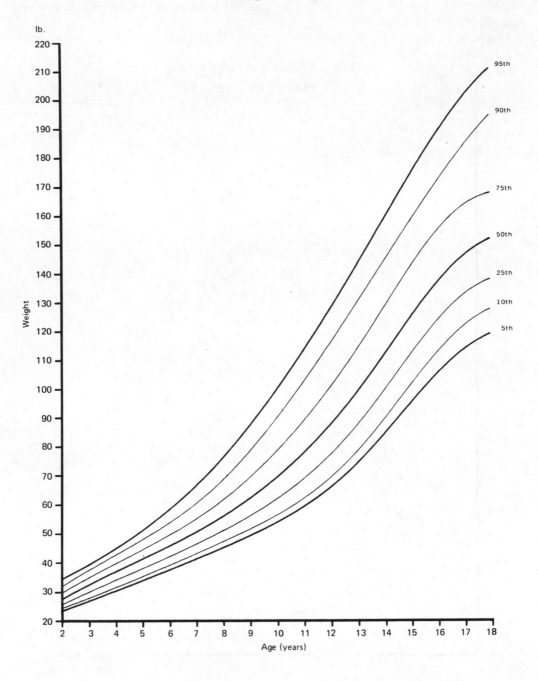

BOYS FROM 2 TO 18 YEARS
Stature for Age

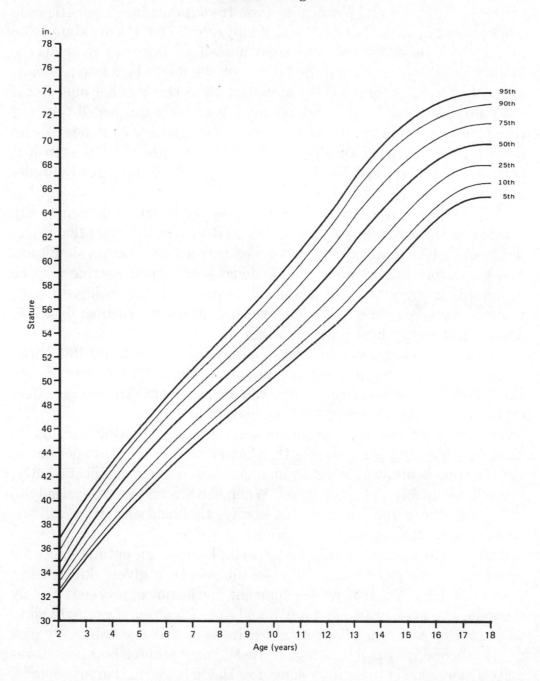

termined by genes and physical factors. If your daughter's genetic code has her programmed to be tall and skinny, she'll be tall and skinny. She might shoot up early and embarrass herself by towering over all the kids in her class—including the boys!—or she might be a late bloomer, reaching her full height a little later than other children her age. But if she's programmed for tall and skinny, it's unlikely that she'll turn out to be short and plump. (Of course, other factors besides genes can influence growth. A careful diet can help to minimize obesity even if it runs in the family. But for the most part, growth is genetically predetermined.)

It is not always easy to separate those predetermined, genetically controlled factors from learned behavior. Research indicates that many behaviors we once thought were learned may actually have a significant genetic factor. For instance, the tendency toward bed-wetting may be inherited, as may the "habit" of nail-biting. And psychologists have realized for some time that some learning disorders, such as dyslexia, are at least partly hereditary in origin.

So how Joanie grows and what abilities she develops are influenced jointly by heredity, environment, and experience. This means that as she follows her personal timetable, you as the parent can have an effect on the rate of development—within certain limits.

You can help her learn to tie her own shoes by showing her how to do it (the learning process) and then by letting her try it (experience), but if Joanie is not yet physically able to manipulate small objects deftly, she will be unable to tie her shoes. When she has matured physically to the point where she achieves that ability, then and only then will she be able to do the job herself.

This is true of mental abilities as well. There is an optimum age for acquiring some intellectual skills—a time when a given skill is most easily acquired. Vocabulary development, for instance, proceeds rapidly between the ages of two and a half and five. Children of normal ability who are exposed to a bilingual environment at that age will easily pick up the second language. (Bilingual Rosalie may achieve both languages a little more slowly than single-language David learns his language skills, but Rosalie will learn both of her languages equally well.) Learning a second language in high school takes much longer because the years between fourteen and eighteen are not the best time to acquire language skills.

It is also true that if Joanie is blocked from learning a skill at the optimum time, she may have trouble picking up the skill at a later date.

Take Jason Evans, for instance (see chapter 1). He suffered a hearing loss that went undetected from the age of three to the age of five—the period of rapid vocabulary expansion. Because he couldn't hear well, he was unable to achieve full development of his language skills. And even though his hearing problem was eventually detected and corrected, he could not easily catch up to where he should have been in language skills. He had passed the peak period for learning to acquire language, and it had a long-term effect on his fluency.

TIMETABLES FOR CHILDREN BORN PREMATURELY

We have said before that each child matures on his or her own schedule, and that the timetables we offer cover a wide range of normal behavior. But there is one group of children who bear special mention when it comes to development: those who were born prematurely.

Because these children have suffered a setback right from the beginning, having lost the advantage of those extra weeks of protected growth and development in the uterus, developmental psychologists expect them to be slower in development for a time.

In fact, psychologists estimate that to get a rough idea of how much a prematurely born child may lag behind his age group, you must double or triple the number of months of prematurity. In other words, a child born two months early will be, not two months behind the other children of that age, but four to six months behind. And in the first five years of life, four to six months can make quite a difference. After all, six months is half a year. So if Joanie was born prematurely, expect her to be acquiring the skills of a slightly younger child than her chronological age indicates.

Before we attempt to describe the course of development for children from three through five, we must double-underline the idea of individual differences. Children are as individual as snowflakes. Though a blizzard looks like just so many white dots, on close inspection each flake is unique, complex, and different.

And among the differences in every area, the differences in temperament stand out. Some children are compliant and steady; others stutter, are overactive, or aggressive; still others are slow to warm up, inexpressive, or hesitant. Life has places for all these individuals as they grow. They need mostly affection and acceptance and a fair but gently guiding hand from parents who accept the task of patient support and caring for the long years till the child reaches maturity. There are no shortcuts, no returns for a new child under the one-year warranty. Your child is a full-fledged participant in life. Your job is to show him how to accept himself—and life.

From Three to Five—An Itinerary

The course of growth and development doesn't run smoothly. In fact, it's a little like being in a small sailboat whose captain (your child!) doesn't know the ropes. You journey onward, and for a few months it's smooth sailing. Then you hit squally weather and are blown backward for a while until the captain regains control. Onward for a few more months, and then suddenly, reefs ahead! Back to more familiar water again until the captain is ready to surge forward. Captain and crew press on in this way, making haste slowly, until gradually the opposite shore comes into view. But even though the captain has never sailed the course before, these waters are not entirely uncharted. Through years of observation, psychologists have established a sequence of maturation that most children follow. As we said before, children travel the route on their own schedule—but they all pass the same landmarks in roughly the same sequence.

So here's a general itinerary for the trip from three to five. Remember,

there is a wide range of development in the area we call "normal." Your Joanie may be either at the top of that range or at the bottom and be perfectly "all right." She may even be outside of the range in some areas and still be doing fine. Also, the fact that she may be slower or faster than "normal" in acquiring a particular skill should not be taken as an indication that she will be similarly fast or slow in acquiring all skills.

THE TWO-AND-A-HALF-YEAR-OLD

A two-and-a-half-year-old child is an "unguided missile." Take Katie! She is the exception to the rule that says you can't move in two directions at one time. Somehow she does it—and she falls down in both directions.

Her instinctive answer to any question is "No."

"Do you want to go to bed?" "No!"

"Do you want me to read you a story?" "No!"

"Do you want a cookie?" "*No!*" (But she's reaching out for it at the same time!)

At this age, most children have trouble relaxing. It seems that they have acquired so much new knowledge and so many exciting skills (what can be headier than the discovery that you can stack three blocks!) that they don't know how to put it all together. They have to keep moving—testing everything, trying everything—until they finally run out of energy.

A two-and-a-half-year-old has certain rituals and is unhappy if they are not followed. Orange juice *before* toast, not after; always the same song at bedtime, and the same routine. Katie insists that her mother say, "Good night, Chicken Little," to which Katie's response is always "Good night, Chicken Big!" If her mother forgets, Katie reminds her—sometimes calling her back from halfway down the stairs to perform the ritual.

A two-and-a-half-year-old is a creature of extremes. One moment she's playing sweetly with a friend; the next minute she's pushing her friend off the swing. At lunchtime, she loves carrots; at dinner she hates them. And just when you think you've been saddled with the most exasperating kid on the face of the earth, she sails into the calm waters of the three-year-old.

THE THREE-YEAR-OLD

The three-year-old's missile system is beginning to develop some guidance. Improved large-muscle control enables her to interact with the house and the outside world with greater confidence—and her improved coordination and control indicate the development of gross and fine motor skills.

At three, Katie has a vocabulary of about nine hundred words, and she uses it confidently. Instead of simply responding to what you say to her or expressing her own needs, she uses language to initiate conversations and ask questions. Seeing her father with ladder, paint, and brushes, she's curious. "Whatcha gonna go an' try an' do?" she asks.

Katie is ahead of her same-aged friend Peter in language development and coordination, and she is behind him in physical strength. This is probably caused partly by inherent physical differences between boys and girls and partly by cultural expectations. Little girls are encouraged to solve problems verbally, while little boys are allowed to use physical strength. As Peter and Katie grow older, Peter will catch up to Katie in language skills, and though Katie may always be slightly better-coordinated than Peter, he will probably remain the stronger. This is the pattern followed by most boys and girls.

Three-year-old Katie is observant and is interested in people. This, in combination with a clear, carrying voice, can prove embarrassing in the supermarket: "Look at that lady, Dad. Why is she so fat?"

A three-year-old's interest in other people applies particularly to children. When you're out shopping and your son disappears, you'll probably find him a few feet away staring at someone else's child, who is staring back with equal interest. They may never speak to each other, but they're enjoying each other nonetheless.

At three, the imagination is developing—as you will notice when you watch your child play. Most of the time three-year-olds engage in what is called *parallel play*. Katie and Peter, playing together, will sit close to each other, but Katie is playing with blocks, building a highway, while Peter has his clown doll and is putting on a circus.

"Now the truck goes up the hill," Katie reports.

"He's standing on his head," Peter says, making his clown do a flip.

"Crash! The truck runs off the road."

"Now he's chasing the doggie."

"The police car comes to help."

"Now the doggie is chasing the clown."

This kind of conversation is typical of three-year-olds. It sounds as if they're talking to each other, but all they're really doing is describing their own actions. They are not unaware of each other, though, and in a few minutes the doggie may begin to chase the police car or the clown may ride in the truck. This is the beginning of cooperative play. But don't expect it to last long—in a few moments, Katie will grab the clown, and Peter will shriek in fury and grab it back. Sharing is not part of a three-year-old's vocabulary.

One of the best things about three-year-olds is that they are anxious to please their parents. At this age Katie wants to be like Mommy and Peter wants to be like Daddy, and they are both attentive and cooperative. They no longer have to be physically restrained from doing something you don't want them to do. They will respond to your spoken words. You might even begin to dream that your child will someday turn into a reasonably pleasant adult. Hold on to that dream, because stormy seas are ahead: a three-and-a-half-year-old is not easy to live with.

THE THREE-AND-A-HALF-YEAR-OLD

At three and a half, kids once again become oppositional. Peter's teacher sees him climbing up on the sink and tells him not to. Peter calmly eyes his teacher—who is still watching him—and proceeds to climb up on the sink anyway.

Three-and-a-half-year-olds can be demanding and hard to please—and very independent. "You don't have to help me," Katie informs her mother, who is trying to help fasten the seat belt in the car. "I'm strong to do it." And although it takes several minutes of figuring and effort, Katie does do it herself.

At this age, kids want to control every situation, from play ("Let's play doctor. I'll be the doctor, and you be the patient." "No, I'm the doctor. You can be the mommy, and Janey can be the patient.") to bedtime ("I won't go to bed unless you read me two stories."). It seems that three-and-a-half-year-old Katie's main concern is to strengthen her will, making this an exhausting time for that primary authority figure, Mother. But Katie and Peter are also creative and sensitive to the feelings of others. (Katie's mom is reading her *Curious George*. The little monkey falls overboard, and Katie is worried. "When I be in the book, I'll save him," she says.)

The omnipotent stage, when the child acts as though the world should be under her control and do just as she wishes, is a crucial one. Omnipotent behavior can reappear again and again in later stages and wreak havoc with the child's ability to come to terms with interpersonal and social demands. Parents need to firmly but gently and lovingly help the three-and-a-half-year-old over this hurdle so that it does not become a set pattern recurring at later developmental stages. Set limits and stick by them. Avoid harsh, punitive stances that pitch you and your child into power struggles. Patiently repeat your expectations, and remember the big, firm parental hug that removes the child from willful behavior. You can help your child accept the world the way it is—frequently not bendable to the child's will, but safe and satisfying nevertheless.

THE FOUR-YEAR-OLD

At four years, kids are shifting into high gear physically. They take great joy in their motor skills, and they love to run and jump and climb and ride a trike and express themselves physically. When Peter is happy, it takes at least three big jumps and a somersault to express his feelings—and when he's mad, he can make the whole house shake. His command over his body is improving rapidly. In fact, the skill that gives him the most trouble right now is standing still!

Friends are becoming more important as socialization skills improve. At four, Katie understands the fairness of sharing. When Peter says, "Katie, can I have one of the horses? You got two and I got none," she is perfectly willing to let Peter play with the palomino while she keeps the spotted pony.

Imagination really begins to fly at this age. Alison, a bright child who is beginning to take an interest in how the body works, knows what the bloodstream is for. Nonetheless, she develops an incredible imaginary theory. "All these mice live inside us, and they carry the food to the toes, and they pick up the BMs and take them away." To illustrate, she traces her own body on a large piece of brown wrapping paper and draws pictures of mice in elevators going up and down inside her legs, carrying buckets full of nameless materials to be properly disposed of.

At four, children begin to realize that there is this thing called death, and that when something has died, it can never come back again. Naturally, this is a fearful concept, and one that takes some dealing with. "Where do dead people go?" asks Jane. "How do they get there—by bus or car? Who carries them?" And—most fearsome thought of all— "Mom, are you going to go away, too?"

They are also full of wonder and curiosity about birth. "I'm going to be a mommy when I grow up," Katie announces importantly. She knows a baby grows in the mother's belly, and she knows it comes out in a special place. She likes having this knowledge—it puts her one up on her younger friends.

A four-year-old is one of the most conceited animals under the sun. "I can draw better than you can," Peter tells Katie. "No, you can't" is her snappy comeback. "I can draw better!!!" Who are they trying to impress? Themselves. They're really not so sure of their ability to cope with life, but by verbally asserting their superiority, they partially convince themselves of their own worth.

Another way four-year-old Katie and Peter make themselves feel competent is to challenge authority. "You aren't the boss of me!" Peter storms at his teacher.

Katie is no longer willing to submit tamely to discipline. When her mother finds it necessary to send her to bed early for some piece of misbehavior, Katie makes her feelings known. From her bed she growls tearfully, "You ruined my favorite day!"

THE FIVE-YEAR-OLD

At five, Katie is quite the little adult. She loves to be given responsibilities around the house—dusting or setting the table. Peter too is cooperative—to the extent of becoming angry if someone else wipes the table after dinner. "That's my job!" They are responsive to praise, looking for approval from the adults around them, and they are particularly dependent on Mom.

There's not as much running and jumping now. A five-year-old is calmer than a four-year-old. Katie is developing an interest in books. She can't read yet, but she imitates her older sister, taking a book off the shelf and looking contentedly at the pictures for several minutes.

That's not to say that physical activities are of no interest. Katie has a new pair of skates and a bike, and she is proud of her skill on both—although for a while her mother was buying Band-Aids by the case.

One of Peter's favorite indoor activities is puppet shows. His long-suffering parents must spend at least fifteen minutes each evening sitting on the living-room floor while Peter and any friends he can rope into the act hide behind the sofa, holding dolls and puppets up on the "stage." At this point, the plays have no structure—indeed, they are likely to consist almost entirely of one character saying hello to another character, hitting him over the head, and whisking off. But Peter never tires of these dramatic evenings.

At five, kids move confidently through their world, feeling secure and capable. However, they generally do have some fears and anxieties. Katie has to have her bedroom door open and the hall light on at night. Kristin doesn't like to have a closed door between her and her mother—not even when Mother is taking a bath. Jimmy is afraid of dogs—a common childhood fear. Jack has an imaginary friend named Jerpy who shares his lonely moments and is always available to take the blame when things go wrong. But Jerpy is not long for this world, because as Jack takes a greater interest in reality, he has less need of imaginary friends.

For the five-year-old, in general, all's right with the world. This is a consolidation period—a resting space before the great stride is taken into the world of the six-year-old.

A GLIMPSE OF THE FUTURE

At six, Peter staunchly maintains that he's "not a little kid anymore"—and he's right. He and Katie are both moving out into the world. They'll become part of a group of friends at school, and as they relate more to their peers, they'll become less dependent upon adults. Their parents will sometimes look back fondly on the two-, three-, or four-year-old who is gone forever, but they'll learn to admire—and wonder at—the individual who is developing under their eyes. The process of growing up is also a process of growing away—away from old needs and dependencies, toward a new selfhood. There's still a long way to go before Peter and Katie are ready to function under their own responsibility, but their feet are on the path, and their parents have set them going in the right direction.

SOME ADDITIONAL NOTES ON SPECIAL TOPICS

Birth and sex. Interest in birth and sex is very common in the preschool years. If this curiosity is met with simple but factual answers, the way is paved for later communication between parent and child when the issues are more complex.

Keep your answers focused on their specific questions. Don't try to provide more information than your child of three, four, or five is looking for. (Remember the old story about the little boy who asked, "Mommy, where did I come from?" His mother launched into a careful description of conception and birth, and at the end, she said, "Does that answer your question?" "No," replied her bewildered boy. "Jimmy comes from Pittsburgh, and I just wanted to know where I came from.")

If you're not quite sure what information your Joanie is looking for, ask what she thinks the answer might be. Keeping your own answers clear and simple—and using correct labels for body parts—is a good rule of thumb.

Your answer can be supplemented by the numerous good books for children and parents on the subject of birth and sex.

Death. Parents, in their struggle to answer questions about death in a gentle manner, frequently euphemize: "Grandpa went away" or "Aunt Martha has gone to sleep forever." Although the intentions are good, this type of response can cause more problems than it solves. It may generate fears about going on trips or going to sleep at night. The preschooler might generalize this concept and become anxious whenever his parents leave the house. If Grandpa went on a long trip and never came back again, can you blame Peter for not wanting to let his father take a business trip to Omaha? As far as Peter is concerned, Omaha might just be another word for death.

How parents actually define death is really a matter of personal belief. Passing along your ideas about death slowly and in a simple manner is a good approach. But be prepared—once a child becomes more aware of the concept of death, it will probably crop up frequently in his play. This is a child's way of dealing with any concept. Don't mistake it for callousness. It's natural, and probably healthy.

Although Joanie may understand that death is final, she may still not understand that it is inevitable. In dealing with the inevitability of death, be truthful but reassuring. "Everybody has to die sometime, but most people and animals don't die until they're really old—*much* older than you or I are." It is also important to reassure her that people don't always die when they get sick. You need to make a distinction between sickness that leads to death and ordinary illnesses, or your child may worry needlessly over every sniffle and headache the family suffers.

Divorce. The process of divorce is difficult for everyone involved, both adults and children. It demands a major adjustment and often generates significant stress and feelings of insecurity, guilt, and worry. The preschooler may experience difficulty sleeping, or he may cry a great deal. He may become withdrawn, or very aggressive. How any child is affected depends a great deal on how the parents manage their relationships with each other and with their children. It is also important to understand that the demands of divorce require that many different needs of the child be met over an extended period of time. Divorce is not a single isolated event in a child's life but rather a series of problems. These may include (1) the predivorce turmoil/reconciliation/turmoil cycle; (2) the separation and divorce itself; (3) the changes resulting in everyday routines; (4) the ongoing demands of being in a single-parent family; and perhaps (5) remarriage.

When parents are divorcing, the preschooler is likely to feel some responsibility for what is happening to the family. Joanie may not be able to put it into words, but the underlying feeling may be "I was bad, and now Daddy is going away." Since preschoolers generally perceive the world to revolve around them, they believe that in some way they have caused the problem. Parents can help to minimize this feeling by making it clear that the divorce is not the child's fault, that the problems belong to the parents.

Another issue that needs a great deal of attention concerns the child's understanding of the future: Where will she live? Will Mommy and Daddy still love her? If divorcing parents can focus on the fact that the children will always be *their children*, it may be easier to work together on clarifying the questions regarding the future. This is a very difficult task because parents are usually very angry at each other at this stage and have a hard time communicating. Much unhappiness, both for the parents and the children, can be avoided if these issues of custody, visitation, and the like are worked out with minimal conflict. It may be helpful for the parents to obtain the services of a trusted third party to accomplish this. It may also be helpful to seek a support group for the children with other children whose parents are divorced. This enables the children to begin to develop an understanding that they have shared feelings and experiences with others their age. That alone reduces some of the upset surrounding the divorce.

Death and divorce can have such a powerful impact upon development that they may profoundly affect the observing process; professional guidance in interpreting your findings is strongly advised. You may, if you are under the stress of a divorce, or any other type of stress, want to take the "Stress Test for Parents" on pages 43–44. If your stress level is too high, you may want to put off testing your child; your stressed state may influence your child's performance on the games.

Discipline. Through our approaches to discipline, we let our children know how we do and don't want them to behave. We let them know directly, through words and actions, that hitting people is not acceptable, and that sharing things with friends *is* acceptable. We also show them indirectly, through our own behaviors: we provide a model of behavior for dealing with feelings, morals, and values.

"What's the best way to discipline a preschooler?" "Is it okay to spank?" "How long should I deny privileges?" These are a few of the questions parents frequently ask. Although it is important to consider each child's need for discipline as well as each parent's style of parenting, research in the area has provided a practical framework regarding discipline.

This framework focuses on the idea that a child can control her own behavior without being afraid of punishment. If a parent values the development of self-control, this can be an effective philosophy of discipline. You can help Joanie to understand how her behavior affects others, and encourage her to be responsible for her behavior. "The reason Jimmy went home was that he didn't have any toys to play with, because you kept them all for yourself. If you'd like Jimmy to come back, why don't you go and tell him that he can play with the dump truck while you use the trailer?"

This technique might be effectively incorporated with such approaches as *response cost* and *time out*. In response cost, if Joanie misbehaves on the swing set, she loses the privilege of playing on the swings for a period of time. The misbehavior costs the child the opportunity to use the swing. Time out, such as sitting on the stairs for a few minutes alone, refers to the removal of the child from a situation in which reinforcers for an inappropriate behavior are accessible. (If Joanie is sitting alone on the stairs, no one is there to notice or pay attention to her temper tantrum.)

These are nonhurtful punishments that avoid the negative side effects of hurtful punishment (spanking or yelling, for instance). The side effects include increasing aggression in the child and providing a negative role model.

When you discipline your child, keep in mind these vital points:

1. Any technique becomes less effective in altering behaviors if it is delayed. Avoid the "wait till your father gets home" syndrome. Not only does it make Dad out to be a bad guy, but by the time Dad comes home, Joanie has probably forgotten what she did wrong.
2. Be consistent. Inconsistent discipline makes behavior more resistant to change. If Joanie knows you don't always punish her for teasing her sister, she'll be willing to keep on doing it on the chance that nothing will happen.
3. Match the punishment to the behavior. If Joanie has been misusing

her bicycle, don't take away television privileges for two weeks. There are two things wrong with this. First, misusing the bike has nothing at all to do with watching television. It is arbitrary and unfair, and Joanie won't learn anything except that adults wield power unfairly. Second, the duration of the punishment is excessive; chances are you won't be able to make yourself follow through on it. A more effective approach would be to take away bike-riding privileges for the remainder of the morning and have Joanie try again later.

4. In order for children to develop self-discipline, it is essential for them to understand the reason for the punishment. "I'm taking away the shovel because you hit Marty with it. Hitting is no good, Joanie."

5. It is often helpful, particularly with preschoolers, to confirm their understanding of rules. For example, this can be accomplished through reminders and clarifying statements. "No bouncing the ball in the house, Joanie. That means basketballs *and* tennis balls. Balls are for outdoors."

□5□

Self-Help Skills

When Sarah's mother and father brought her home from the hospital, flushed with pride and full of enthusiasm, the last thought in their minds was that they were going to spend the next three years of their lives doing absolutely everything for this little individual. When they carried her into the house, they never thought that in a year she was going to be remarkably heavy and would still need to be carried. When they put on her first clean sleeper, they had no vision of the number of times they were going to thrust that same small arm into one sleeve or another. When they first succeeded in convincing her that a spoon was almost as good as a bottle, they didn't stop to think that for many months to come, they would have to place every spoonful of food into that little mouth.

But by the time Sarah was almost three, they were asking themselves at least once a day, "Isn't she *ever* going to learn to put her own snowsuit on, button her own sweater, brush her own teeth, *use the toilet?*"

You're probably asking the same questions. Cheer up. The answer is "Yes. Soon."

SELF-HELP FROM THREE TO FIVE

When she was three, Sarah did begin to use her spoon with some skill. She wasn't very neat about it, but at least her mother didn't have to sit there and guide every spoonful into her mouth. And when the meal was over, with just a little help she could wash her own hands and face—

which badly needed washing—and dry her hands on a towel. She could even be trusted to know which was the hot-water faucet and which was cold.

When it came to getting dressed, three-year-old Sarah was no longer a passive doll who had to be manipulated into her shirt and jeans. She could get her own arms into her sleeves and pull up her pants herself. She was also good at taking her jeans off all by herself. (In fact, she once performed this chore in the hardware department of the Sears store while her father was concentrating on paint samples.) Best of all, she knew what the toilet was for and could urinate by herself—if someone helped her get her overalls unhooked and pulled down in time.

When she was four, Sarah had acquired some new skills that made life a little easier for her parents. She could feed herself fairly neatly, using a fork, and she could spread her own butter with a knife—if the butter were soft. If she spilled, she could wipe it up herself. In fact, she enjoyed it. She could brush her own teeth and only needed to be watched to see that she didn't use six inches of toothpaste for one brushing. She could pretty much dress herself, with a little supervision and some help with the buttons. She could even put on her own socks. She could take off her own T-shirt, too. This was helpful at bedtime, but frustrating when she did it during the day and left the shirt "I dun know where."

There was progress in the bathroom, too. Sarah was now able to do almost everything by herself. She still needed help with one thing, though: "I need a wipe!" she would yell, and her mother or father would have to stop what they were doing and go to the bathroom, where they would find their daughter patiently waiting, head down, bottom up, for that one step she couldn't quite manage on her own.

Emancipation came when Sarah was five. At last she was able to take care of *all* her toileting needs. In fact, she could keep herself clean and brushed all by herself, as long as someone reminded her—and reminded her, and reminded her.

At five, Sarah could be trusted to cut her own food with a table knife. When it came to getting dressed, she could almost do it all. She knew which shoe went on which foot, and she could zip her own jacket. She only needed help tying her shoes. At bedtime, she could get undressed and into her pajamas completely unassisted—if she wanted to.

As you keep track of your own child's progress in self-help skills, you'll find that, though he may do some things faster or slower than Sarah, he will probably follow the same sequence. It's largely a matter of growing ability in motor skills plus visual abilities that enable the growing child to perceive what needs to be done and how things fit together. Sarah had to be able to match the shape of her foot to the shape of her shoe before she could put the right shoe on the right foot, and she had to be able to manipulate the shoelaces in a specific perceived pattern before she could tie her shoes—a task most children don't master until they are five and a half or six.

SELF-HELP ACTIVITIES

In identifying your child's self-help skills, it will probably not be necessary to set up situations for observation. Most if not all of these skills are part of your daily routines. All you have to do is read over the list of skills so you'll know what to watch for, then keep an eye on your child throughout the day to see how she performs the listed tasks. Let her try each task unassisted before you step in to offer help. Provide frequent demonstrations, and let your child attempt to complete parts of the total skill. Recognize effort and encourage attempts at independence regarding skill completion. Reinforce progress made. This is a good time to remind you that having your child practice a skill that he or she is having difficulty with or is not ready for will not help the child gain the skill sooner and may create more problems. Practice those skills that your child is just about ready to master. This will build self-confidence and strengthen the learning process.

	Age		
	3½	4½	5½

FEEDING

	3½	4½	5½
1. Child eats skillfully with a spoon	☐	☐	☐
2. Child feeds self with little spilling	☐	☐	☐
3. Child pours from a pitcher	⬚	☐	☐
4. Child spreads butter with a knife	⬚	☐	☐
5. Child eats with a fork	⬚	☐	☐
6. Child cuts with a knife	⬚	⬚	☐

DRESSING

	3½	4½	5½
1. Child assists in dressing	☐	☐	☐
2. Child puts on coat unassisted	☐	☐	☐
3. Child removes "pull-down" garments (pants, skirts)	☐	☐	☐
4. Child removes "pull-over" garments (shirts, sweaters)	⬚	☐	☐
5. Child dresses self with supervision	⬚	☐	☐
6. Child puts on socks	⬚	☐	☐
7. Child knows which shoe goes on which foot	⬚	⬚	☐
8. Child zips front zipper	⬚	⬚	☐
9. Child dresses self without assistance except for tying	⬚	⬚	☐

(Continued on next page)

	Age		
	3½	4½	5½

GROOMING

	3½	4½	5½
1. Child washes face with assistance	☐	☐	☐
2. Child knows hot and cold faucets	☐	☐	☐
3. Child dries own hands	☐	☐	☐
4. Child brushes teeth with assistance	☐	☐	☐
5. Child brushes teeth unassisted	☐	☐	☐
6. Child washes face and hands unassisted	☐	☐	☐
7. Child bathes with minimal assistance	☐	☐	☐
8. Child brushes hair	☐	☐	☐

TOILETING

	3½	4½	5½
1. Child urinates without assistance	☐	☐	☐
2. Child cares for toileting needs other than wiping	☐	☐	☐
3. Child assumes total care for toileting needs	☐	☐	☐

MISCELLANEOUS

	3½	4½	5½
1. Child helps put things away	☐	☐	☐
2. Child puts away toys himself	☐	☐	☐
3. Child mops up spills	☐	☐	☐

WHAT TO DO WITH YOUR RESULTS

How does your scoring look for the self-help games and tests? Do you see a lot of pluses? Then your Debbie is farther along the path to independence than most children her age, and you're on your way to emancipation—or, at least, as much emancipation as any parent will ever attain. (Your child won't always need you to tie those shoelaces, but, happily, children seldom completely outgrow their need for Mom and Dad.)

Are there more than a few empty boxes? Then your child is behind others in the same age group for self-help skills.

If you see a lot of checks, with maybe a few pluses and some empty boxes, then Debbie is typical of her age group. Hang in there. Sooner or later, she will learn to button her own sweater and put away her own toys.

If Debbie scores low in self-help *and* in other areas, such as learning and general information or language, this may be an indication of a learning difficulty, and you will want to seek professional help.

As usual, begin with your nursery-school teacher, and then, if concern is warranted, look for help from specialists. It's unlikely that your pediatrician will be able to help you analyze Debbie's self-help abilities; he or she doesn't really see enough of her to be of much help here. However, the doctor may be able to recommend a specialist—perhaps a child development team or a child psychologist—to help you if you are concerned.

There are several possible reasons why your child's development may lag. One—the least likely—is that there may be some retardation involved. Another is that your particular style of parenting has not encouraged Debbie to develop the skills that will lead to greater independence. A third possibility is that Debbie's personality development is not leading her to become responsible; sometimes little kids want to stay little, and they resist acquiring the skills that will help them develop independence.

So the first question to ask of anybody is one you can ask of yourself: "Is there anything in our child-rearing style or strategy that might be hindering the development of self-help skills?" Some situations that have been known to hinder self-help skills: children who must be left alone much of the time or who are raised to a large degree by an older sibling, and children who are overprotected and cosseted. (Often loving parents see it as a way of expressing affection: Katie's mother beckons her over and buttons her sweater while giving her a kiss, in spite of Katie's protests that she can do it herself. Katie's mother would be wise to content herself with giving the kid a kiss and letting her button her own sweater.)

It sometimes happens that children who are overly dependent when their parents are around may be quite self-sufficient when Mom and Dad are not at hand. So if you're concerned, check it out with the nursery-school teacher. Does Debbie put on her own boots and zip her jacket at nursery school? Does she put her dishes in the sink when the other kids do? Does she hang her coat up in her cubby, or does she drop it and expect someone else to put it away for her?

Another thing to check with the teacher: *Should* Debbie be putting her own dishes in the sink and putting on her own boots, or are these tasks not yet expected of children her age? Sometimes parents can expect too much of a child, particularly a first child. It's easy for adults to forget how hard it was to learn to tie your shoes. The teachers probably have a better grasp of what to expect of three-and-a-half-year-olds than you do, even though you do know your own specimen better than the teachers do.

Or you might find that you're expecting too little of Debbie. If you don't know that a four-year-old is capable of writing her own name, you might not have offered her the opportunity to try it. Perhaps all that's needed is to give your child the opportunity to try things for herself—a little *before* you think she would be able to succeed. Give the kid a chance to stretch. If we never try anything we're not absolutely capable of doing, we miss our chances to grow.

So if your child is having difficulties in self-help but not in other areas, the problem is probably a matter of parenting style or personality factors. The important thing to do in this case is to try to change those factors that you think may be responsible. You may be able to find guidance from a child psychologist in this endeavor. Or you may find it helpful to enroll in one of the many parenting classes offered in most communities by church groups, YMCAs, and schools. Your nursery school may even sponsor workshops or seminars in parenting.

Another clue that you should pay attention to is if Debbie *had* some skills but seems to have lost them. It's important to know if what you're seeing is a regression. If regression is involved, you should ask yourself if there have been any stresses that might be causing the child to temporarily backslide. Divorce, loss of employment, a new baby, moving—these are things that can cause the most independent child to seek the comfort and security that she may find in being cosseted like a baby. You may be able to work things out by showing Debbie extra love and understanding—but *not* by relaxing your expectations that she button her own shirt and pour her own milk—until she feels secure enough to move ahead again. Giving in to her demands that you feed and dress her will only prolong the situation. Stick to your guns, but give her plenty of love, and you'll probably all come though the bad patch with no serious ill effects.

It is worth noting, however, that a regression that *isn't* temporary—that lasts three months or more—is a serious matter; professional help is definitely warranted.

Montessori schools are particularly strong in developing self-help skills, so if you are looking for a school, and if self-help skills are important to you, you might want to check into the one in your community.

Encourage your child's self-help skills by permitting her to help out around the house. Let her take on the responsibility of emptying the silverware basket of the dishwasher or putting the napkins on the dinner table, or, if she is older, let her set the table by herself. Let your child know that she is capable of helping out, and that you appreciate her help. Expect her to help you clean her room and, as she grows older, to take on more and more of this responsibility herself—and let your child *know* that you expect this of her.

In teaching Debbie a new skill, first show her how to do it. Words aren't as helpful as demonstrations. Do it on yourself, slowly, explaining what you are doing. (Don't expect one demonstration to do the trick. You'll probably have to repeat the moves a few times.) Ask her to do what you are doing. Watch how she does it, and if she has problems, repeat your demonstration. The more often she copies what you show her, the better she will be able to do the job.

You can spread your demonstration out over several sessions to help her grasp the entire project. For instance, if you're expecting her to put her own belt on sometime soon, start out by putting her belt on all the way except for the last belt loop. Have Debbie do that one. Soon she will be able to thread the belt through two loops, then all of them. Taking it one step at a time breaks the job down into bite-size pieces that the child can easily swallow.

Another clue: If you're trying to show your child how to hold scissors, don't manipulate her hand or try to thread the fingers through the handle. Instead, demonstrate: hold the scissors properly yourself, let your child look carefully, then let her get her own hand into the right position. She will learn better if she does it by herself.

Also, make it easy for Debbie to succeed by thinking ahead to avoid pitfalls. If you want her to carry a glass of milk from the kitchen to the dining room, don't fill the glass full, or we guarantee she'll spill it. That's just asking too much of pint-size motor skills. Fill it half full, and ensure success.

For play-practice in getting dressed, there are Dressy Bessy and Dapper Dan dolls whose clothing buttons, laces, zips, and ties—with big buttons, laces, and eyelets that are easy for small, unskilled fingers to manipulate.

Often children will complain that they just can't do it. This is frequently a bid for encouragement, support, and more demonstrations. Don't give up, and don't let your child give up. Offer the support and provide the demonstrations, along with your confidence that soon she will lick this problem. Victory will come. Very few thirty-year-olds need their mothers to button their pajamas for them!

□6□

Learning and General Information

When an infant is born, his mind is blank. Reflexes rule him. When something warm touches one-day-old Tyler's cheek, he automatically turns toward it, and lo! something nice happens: he is fed. He doesn't know what or how or who. He doesn't even know that there *is* a what or a how or a who. He's a *tabula rasa*—a blank slate—an empty vessel waiting to be filled, not just with milk, but with knowledge.

A few months later, Tyler has learned a few things. Somehow, he has absorbed what goes on around him—sights, smells, tastes, sounds, sensations—and he has turned them into meaningful experiences. He now knows that there is a what, a how, and a who. He cries when he's hungry; when he sees the bottle he reaches for it and drains it eagerly; he even knows that he prefers one person over all others. He'll cry when she leaves the room, and stop crying when she comes into the room.

A few years later, Tyler is into computer programming.

Truly, learning is an ongoing miracle!

It is our tremendous capacity to learn that makes humans uniquely human. No other animal has the capability to learn abstract concepts the way humans do. A cat can learn to come running at the sound of a can opener; a chimpanzee can learn to use sign language; but only a human can learn to study how learning takes place.

Through observation and testing, we have learned much about how learning takes place. We don't know everything, but we do know some of the processes involved and some of the factors that can affect them.

Learning is based on a number of factors:

1. *The capacity to learn.* Intelligence tests were devised in an effort to measure this capacity.

2. *The opportunity to practice.* The more chances Jeremy gets to ride his bicycle, the better he'll be able to do it.

3. *The motivation to learn.* Jeremy is anxious to learn to ride a bike because his best friend already knows how and Jeremy is impressed.

4. *The ability to conceptualize; insight.* There comes a moment when Jeremy finally realizes, "Hey! If I can keep my weight right in the middle, I won't fall off the bike!"

5. *The similarity to things learned previously.* Jeremy already knows how to ride a tricycle, so he can apply that knowledge to riding his bike.

6. *The length of time since the previous knowledge was last used.* Since Jeremy rides his trike every day, the pedal-pushing technique is fresh in his mind and is easily transferred to biking.

7. *Feedback.* Jeremy needs to know what he's doing right and wrong so he can correct his errors. He needs to know that the reason he fell was that he wasn't going fast enough.

8. *Rewards or encouragement.* Students will often work harder if they know they will get something desirable when they succeed. In Jeremy's case, his reward might be the admiration of his peers—but it is quite likely that his greatest reward will be his own pleasure in having achieved his goal. Humans are like that. We tend to enjoy our own accomplishments even better than a reward. Encouragement is often the best reward of all. When Dad says, "Hey, Jeremy! You must feel like quite a little biker. You're really getting a kick out of it!" Jeremy glows with pleasure and redoubles his efforts.

LEARNING PLATEAUS

"When Charlie was three, I thought he was a genius," his mother says. "When he was four, I thought he was very bright. When he was five, I thought he was at least above average. Now that he's six, I think he's just a typical kid."

Did Charlie grow stupid over the years? No—he was just reflecting a typical pattern of learning, one that has as much to do with the way his mother perceived his learning as with Charlie's learning process itself.

When he was an infant—a *tabula rasa*—he knew nothing. The learning process began with the first thing he learned. Then the minute he learned a second thing, he doubled the sum of his knowledge. When he knew four things, he had again doubled his knowledge. Stimuli came fast and furious, and there was plenty of room in Charlie's brain to store everything he learned. Every new skill was a triumph, something to be talked about and demonstrated to Grandma when she came to visit. He soaked up new knowledge as fast as it came along, and he stored it away in his brain, piecemeal. But because he didn't know how to make connections between things, he reached a plateau in his learning. And there he stayed until he had learned to sort out and deal with the information he had gathered. It wasn't that he had grown stupid. He had just passed the stage of life where separate bits of knowledge could be absorbed quickly and easily. Now that he was struggling with learning more complex material, it would take him longer to absorb information because he also had to cross-reference it and figure out how it related to what he already knew.

Most children learn in the same way Charlie did. They absorb new knowledge swiftly for a while. Then they plateau and learn to deal with what they've absorbed. Then they're ready to take in a new batch of information, and for a few months they again seem to make great strides, until they plateau again, consolidating their gains. The older a child gets, the more complex the information he must take in, cutting down on the speed with which he can learn. Look at it this way: you can teach Sharon "The Alphabet Song" in a few minutes; it will take her much longer to learn to read and write.

Speaking of "The Alphabet Song," there you have an excellent example of another reason why children learn so fast in their early years: much of what they have to learn involves simple memorization. When two-year-old Charlie's proud mother asks, "What does a cow say?" Charlie says, "Mooo." It's cute, and it's clever—but Charlie's a city boy, and he has no idea what a cow is. He's just repeating something he has memorized.

When he gets to be five and his nursery school teaches him the Pledge of Allegiance, he memorizes the sounds and parrots them back. But when he gets home he asks his mom, "Who's Richard Sands?"

"What are you talking about?" his bewildered mother responds.

"Richard Sands!" Charlie repeats. Then patiently, "You know—'and to the republic for Richard Sands.' "

Children between three and five have a great ability to do rote memorization—parroting. The ability for integrated learning is a skill that Charlie will develop as he grows older—and naturally, this kind of learning is more difficult. It takes longer to soak up the concept behind the meaning of numbers than it does to memorize "one, two, three, four, five."

Remember the wonderful pumpyard scene in the movie *The Miracle Worker*, when Helen Keller finally realizes the relationship between the word *water* and the cold, wet stuff pouring over her hands? For months she had been memorizing words in the finger alphabet and parroting them back to her teacher—but in that one moment, Helen made the giant step connecting the thing with its symbol. That is the difference between memorizing and learning.

HOW YOU CAN HELP YOUR CHILD LEARN

We don't know yet all there is to know about learning, but we have found out enough about it to realize that certain techniques make learning easier.

Repetition, for instance, enhances learning. That's why your three-year-old is word perfect on the McDonald's commercials, right down to the syncopation.

Incidentally, researchers debate whether it is the process of repetition that causes the brain to learn something, or whether the brain simply grasps the concept all at once upon the last repetition. In that scene from *The Miracle Worker* when Helen finally grasps the concept behind the word *water*, did the months of memorized repetition help Helen to learn inch-by-inch until the understanding was complete—or was it simply that at last, on this particular repetition, her brain was ready to make the connection?

The debate is ongoing—but in a way, it's not a matter that you as parents need to worry about. Because, in either event, repetition is helpful. If it's the process of repetition that does the job bit by bit, fine. But if the brain makes a sudden intuitive leap, then the more often you repeat something, the more likely the brain is to make the leap sooner, simply because the opportunity is presented more often.

Another interesting point to remember is that constant success is *not* the best teacher. The expression "Nothing succeeds like success" is misleading. Charlie learns faster when his efforts meet sometimes with success and sometimes with failure. The failures reinforce the successes—they show what doesn't work as well as what does work. And a large part of learning is knowing not just what's right, but what's wrong. Knowing not merely that "one, two, three, four, five" is correct, but also that *only* "one, two, three, four, five" is correct and that "one, two, four, three, five" is wrong. Knowing that washing your hands before meals is right, and that coming to the table with dirty hands is wrong.

Furthermore, when Charlie fails, he must try again to succeed, and repetition, as we have seen, is an effective teacher. So when you see your Charlie struggling to get up on the seesaw and you hurry to his aid, you haven't really helped him. Leave him alone—let him try and fail, and try and fail, and try and succeed. He'll learn faster, he'll learn better—and he'll be less likely to forget.

During the years from three to five, a child picks up a great deal of general information. When Charlie gets to school, he'll start learning how to read, write, add, subtract, and tell time. Right now he's acquiring information about himself, his life, and his world. This knowledge comes to him a little at a time, in a sequence from simpler facts to the most difficult. Charlie may learn faster or slower than his best friend, Jack, but the likelihood is high that they, like most children, will pick up this knowledge in roughly the same sequence. (Remember, as we discuss general information, that we're not necessarily talking about the skill required to *do* something; we're talking about the knowledge it takes to *talk about* it. Charlie couldn't go to the store alone to buy a carton of milk, but he knows where *you* go to buy it.)

GENERAL INFORMATION— FROM THREE YEARS TO FIVE YEARS

The first bit of personal data Charlie picks up on, naturally enough, is his name. He's got that down well before the age of three. He also begins working on the concept of time at this age. He knows night from day, and he understands that there is such a thing as time. He knows about "waiting" now. No longer does he need instant gratification of his needs; he can be satisfied—for a while—with knowing that his friend Jack will be coming over "soon." But when he's told he can't have a peanut because he's not old enough to chew peanuts thoroughly, he says, "Then can I hold it in my hand until I'm older?" The concept of years has little meaning to him—it's too big a lump of time to get a good grip on. He talks about time in quite an adult way. "Time for lunch," he announces tersely—at nine-thirty in the morning. "What time is it?" he asks—meaning, "Is it time for 'Mr. Rogers' Neighborhood' yet?" But *tomorrow* means any time in the future, and *yesterday* may turn out to be last month or last year. And if you ask him what time it is, you always get the same answer, day or night: "Forty-twelve."

At three, Charlie is learning about his body. He can play "Where's your nose (or toes or elbow)." He can name some of his body parts, although *elbow* always comes out "ellabow." Three-year-old Charlie can also name a few of the animals in his favorite storybooks. If you give him a red block and ask him to find all the other blocks that are the same color, he can do it, but he can't name the colors yet, and when his mother asks him to hand her the blue cushion without showing him an example, he just grabs the cushion closest to him, which happens to be green.

"When I grow up, I'm going to be on TV," says three-and-a-half-year-old Charlie. Then there's a pause—"Except I don't think I'm small enough to fit." Charlie knows something about relative size now, if not very much about television. He has known since he was three which of two things is bigger or smaller, but now he also realizes that big feet can't go into small shoes.

When Charlie is three-and-a-half, he goes trick-or-treating on Halloween with two of his friends, two-and-a-half-year-old Sandy and five-year-old Jack. When the youngsters return to Charlie's house laden with goodies, they have a conversation that tells a lot about the relative abilities of a two-and-a-half-year-old, a three-and-a-half-year-old, and a five-year-old when it comes to dealing with quantities.

"Wow, we got lots!" says Sandy. She has no ability to think in terms of numbers yet.

Charlie starts counting, but he loses track after five and announces with reckless abandon that he has "hundreds of candy!"

Jack, better able to deal with numbers, carefully counts each piece and comes up with an accurate total of twenty-seven pieces of candy in his bag.

Charlie's mother gives each of the children a bowl to put the candy in. But the bowls aren't all the same size. Jack's bowl is smaller than Charlie's—and therefore his twenty-seven pieces of candy fill his bowl to the brim. Meanwhile, Charlie's twenty-seven pieces make a small pile in the bottom of his bigger bowl. Charlie is on the verge of tears. "Jack got more than me!" Jack tries to explain that they have the same amount, but Charlie can't see it. His quick-thinking mother saves the day by switching bowls so that Charlie has the smaller bowl. Thus, Charlie is happy, and Jack, who knew that the size of the bowl didn't affect the amount of candy, didn't mind a bit. (Little Sandy was off in a corner eating her candy and didn't care about the size of the bowl at all.)

At four, Charlie begins to pick up some information about numbers.

He can recite numbers up to five—but when it comes to counting, he misses the one-to-one ratio. He can count and point to one-two-three toy cars—but then the finger loses the place, so he may point to the fourth car and say "four, five. . . ." He doesn't really understand counting yet.

He can show you which is the blue boat and which is the red car, but he can't spontaneously tell you what color his sweater is.

In his fourth year, Charlie knows that he's a boy. He can also tell you how old he is. "Not four—four and a half!" He knows what a bed, a table, a chair, and a refrigerator are for. He knows that a stove is for cooking, and that a coat keeps you warm when it's cold out. And he has, by this time, developed some problem-solving abilities. He knows what people are supposed to do when they're hungry, or cold, or tired.

By the time he's five, Charlie can tell you that his sweater is red and his jeans are blue. He can count to ten, and he can tell a nickel from a dime. (He'd rather have the nickel because it's bigger, so it must be worth more pennies.)

Now he has firmed up his time concepts. He knows that he goes to kindergarten in the morning and comes home in the afternoon. "Yesterday I went to Jack's house, and tomorrow Jack is coming here," he says—and he's using those words accurately.

During the fifth year, Charlie learns right from left—but only *his* right and *his* left. Charlie's father introduces him to a businessman who offers to shake hands, man-to-man, holding out his hand. Charlie shakes his head wisely. "You're supposed to shake with your *right* hand," he says, pointing to the hand opposite Charlie's right. The bemused stranger has to offer his left hand before Charlie will accept it.

At five, Charlie knows his address, and he can tell you not only how old he is but the exact date when he'll be six. He can also tell you the names of his three brothers and sisters. He knows that books are for reading, although he can't read yet himself; he knows that clocks are for telling time, although he can't do that yet, either. And he knows what a pencil is for. He can tell you what to do if your hands are dirty or if you walk into a dark room. He can count to ten, pointing accurately, but he still thinks that the biggest person in the room is the oldest person in the room—he doesn't yet realize that age has to do with time, not size. (He may not get this idea straightened out until he's six or seven.)

He won't be able to remember his telephone number until six, either, and he'll probably be six before he can tell you his parents' names. Also at six, Charlie's problem-solving skills will be slightly more abstract. He will be able to tell you what to do when it's raining or when there is a fire. He'll be able to tell you what to do when you break something. ("Fix it!")

As Charlie grows and develops, he'll add to his store of knowledge, building upon what he already knows to learn more and more—and it really won't be long before he's teaching his mother how to program a computer.

Like Charlie, your child gathers information about herself and the world around her. Her ability to pick up on, to remember, and to use these facts is reflected in what is termed "the fund of general information." The games we've selected will give your child a chance to show you what information she has gathered and how she applies this information in describing her world and solving everyday problems.

The following activities present a number of different types of questions and problems. Your child will answer some questions, do some drawings, look at some pictures, and talk about things found around the house. Some items you could probably fill in without asking your child, but part of the fun of the games is getting and saving the actual words the child uses to answer. So have your child give a response, even if you know that she can do it correctly. This will enable you to see the change in the quality of the answers as your child matures, and it may also provide some memorable responses.

Scoring: Each item is marked with a box at the age that almost all children can respond correctly. Write your child's response on the line, and check the items your child answers correctly. (For general scoring instructions, see pages 45–49.)

GENERAL INFORMATION: SELF-AWARENESS

"ALL ABOUT ME"

The very first awarenesses that the child develops are about himself. These are the facts that are important to the child, and they reflect his first steps in learning.

Let your child know that this is a book about him and how he grows. Tell him that you need his help in starting the book.

Instructions: Say to your child, "I'm going to ask you some questions. Some of the things I ask may be easy, and some you may not know yet. I want to write down which ones you can say—just for fun." Write down your child's response on the line, and score according to the instructions under the line. (For general scoring instructions, see pages 45–49.)

	Age		
	3½	4½	5½

1. "What is your name?" (If child gives first name only, ask for full name.)

3½ _____ ☐

(If child gives first name only, score a check. If child gives first and last, score a plus.)

4½ _____ ☐

(If child gives first and last names, score a check.)

5½ _____ ☐

(If child gives first and last names, score a check.)

(Continued on next page)

	Age		
	3½	4½	5½

2. "Are you a boy or a girl?"

3½ _____ ☐

4½ _____   ☐

5½ _____   ☐

3. "How old are you?" (If child holds up fingers, ask, "How many is that?")

3½ _____ ☐

4½ _____   ☐

5½ _____   ☐

4. "Do you have any brothers or sisters?" (If yes, "How many brothers? How many sisters?" Check this item only if your child can say the *number* of brothers or sisters.)

3½ _____ ☐

4½ _____   ☐

5½ _____   ☐

	Age		
	3½	4½	5½

5. "When is your birthday?"

3½ _____   ☐
(If child gives month, or day and month, score a plus.)

4½ _____   ☐
(If child gives month only, score a check.)

5½ _____   ☐
(If child gives month and day, score a check.)

6. "Where do you live?" (If child gives town, ask, "What street do you live on?")

3½ _____   ☐
(If child gives any part of address, score a plus.)

4½ _____   ☐
(If child gives street or street number only, score a check.)

5½ _____   ☐
(If child gives street and number, score a check.)

(Continued on next page)

	Age		
	3½	4½	5½

7. "What is your phone number?"

3½ _____ ⬚

(If partially correct, score a check.)

4½ _____   ☐

(If partially correct, score a check.
If fully correct, score a plus.)

5½ _____   ☐

(If fully correct, score a check.)

"MY WORLD"

This section is not to be scored. It will give you a chance to watch the development of your child's skill in drawing, and it will also show you something of the details your child is aware of when thinking of your house and family.

Most three-year-olds have limited ability to draw recognizable objects and people, so don't be surprised if the early drawings look like random marks on the paper. (Appendix A presents some sample drawings by three-, four-, and five-year-olds of houses and people.) Give the child paper and pencil and ask him to draw a picture of his house and his family. Clip a photograph of each to your child's drawings, just for the fun of comparing it to the real thing. Collect drawings for all three age levels. (Keep all these papers in a file.)

WHAT'S MISSING?

In gathering general information, the young child begins with an awareness of self and body parts.

Instructions: Photocopy or trace the incomplete drawing of a person on this page and say, "Here's a picture of a person. But some things are missing. Can you put the missing parts on the person?" Give your child the drawing and a pencil. Don't offer any hints as your child works, and don't seem to expect more body parts when she indicates that she is finished. Just accept and score what your child adds to the figure un-prompted.

Samples of how other children completed the picture are shown on pages 98–99. The first drawing presented is for age three; the second is for age three and a half; the third is for age four; and the fourth is for age five.

_____ Mouth

_____ Nose

✓ Eyes

_____ Ears

_____ Arms

_____ Hand, fingers

_____ Leg

_____ Foot

_____ Hair

_____ Neck

_____ Clothing

_____ Other facial detail

Sample of three-year-old's work.

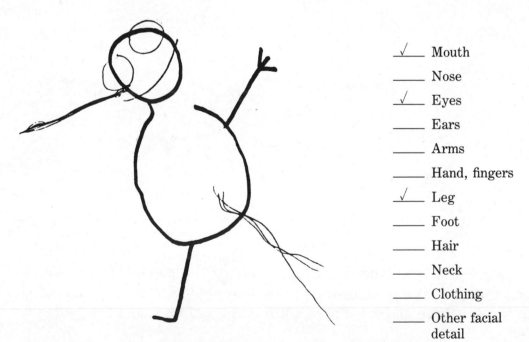

✓ Mouth

_____ Nose

✓ Eyes

_____ Ears

_____ Arms

_____ Hand, fingers

✓ Leg

_____ Foot

_____ Hair

_____ Neck

_____ Clothing

_____ Other facial detail

Sample of three-and-a-half-year-old's work.

√	Mouth
√	Nose
√	Eyes
——	Ears
√	Arms
√	Hand, fingers
√	Leg
√	Foot
√	Hair
√	Neck
√	Clothing
——	Other facial detail

Sample of four-year-old's work.

√	Mouth
√	Nose
√	Eyes
√	Ears
√	Arms
√	Hand, fingers
√	Leg
√	Foot
√	Hair
√	Neck
√	Clothing
√	Other facial detail

Sample of five-year-old's work.

(Continued on next page)

Most three-year-olds will perceive the lack of arms and legs and eyes.

Most four-year-olds will notice, in addition to the above, the need for hands, feet, a neck, and some facial features.

Most five-year-olds will add also facial details, perhaps clothing, possibly fingers.

Many young children will add a belly button, but this is a nonscored item. It is usually left out by four- or five-year-olds.

Your child may perceive the lack of items other than those seen by most children of his age. That's perfectly all right. The score is the same for two eyes and a nose as it is for an arm, a leg, and a foot. (For general scoring instructions, see pages 45–49.)

		Age		
		3½	4½	5½
3½	Child adds three parts	☐		
4½	Child adds five parts		☐	
5½	Child adds seven parts			☐

(If a child adds two parts *more* than indicated, score a plus.)

DRAW A HOUSE

A simple figure that children can draw at a young age, and one that reflects their growing awareness and fund of information, is the house.

Instructions: Say to your child, "Do you know what a house looks like?" If she says yes, say, "Draw a picture of a house." Give her paper and pencil. Score this activity by making a note of the recognizable features your child adds to the basic house shape—a square with a pointed roof. Some of the features preschoolers might add to their house drawings are doors, windows, windowpanes, curtains, a chimney, a TV antenna, a fire escape, a doorbell, and a mailbox. Your child may add other features. (For general scoring instructions, see pages 45–49.)

	Age		
	3½	4½	5½
3½ Child draws three features	☐		
4½ Child draws four features		☐	
5½ Child draws five features			☐

I CAN PRINT MY NAME

Early interest in knowing letters and printing one's name is seen in many children as they move ahead in their pursuit of knowledge and mastery of skills.

Instructions: Ask your child to print her name in the space provided. Since this is not being evaluated as a motor task, mark this item correct even if the line quality is shaky. (For general scoring instructions, see pages 45–49.)

	Age		
	3½	4½	5½
3½ _____ (If child attempts at least first name, score a check. If child prints at least first name with letters all correct, score a plus.)	☐		
4½ _____ (If child attempts at least first name and some letters in last name, score a check. If child gets first name all correct and at least initial of last name, score a plus.)		☐	
5½ _____ (If child attempts first and last name, score a check. If child prints first and last names all correctly, score a plus.)			☐

GENERAL INFORMATION: OBJECT USE

WHAT'S IT FOR?

Much of the thinking and learning that preschoolers do is concerned with things they can touch, hold, and see. Talking about things in their world is a good way for children to show their developing understanding.

Instructions: Tell your child, "I'll name some things that we have in our house. You tell me what they are used for." Don't prompt, even if you think your child knows. If he says, "I don't know," leave the space blank.

Write your child's answers on the lines. As she matures, her answers will become more complete and accurate. (For general scoring instructions, see pages 45–49.)

If your child is unable to answer three or four items in a row, you may want to discontinue this activity to avoid discouragement. Try again in a few months or at the next age level.

	Response	*Age*		
		3½	4½	5½
1. Bed				
3½	_____	☐		
4½	_____		☐	
5½	_____			☐
2. Chair				
3½	_____	☐		
4½	_____		☐	
5½	_____			☐

	Response	Age		
		3½	4½	5½

3. Table

3½	_____	☐		
4½	_____		☐	
5½	_____			☐

4. Glass

3½	_____	☐		
4½	_____		☐	
5½	_____			☐

5. Refrigerator

3½	_____	☐		
4½	_____		☐	
5½	_____			☐

6. Stove

3½	_____	☐		
4½	_____		☐	
5½	_____			☐

(Continued on next page)

Response		*Age*	
	3½	4½	5½

7. Coat

3½ _____ ☐

4½ _____   ☐

5½ _____   ☐

8. Book

3½ _____ ☐

4½ _____   ☐

5½ _____   ☐

9. Pencil

3½ _____ ☐

4½ _____   ☐

5½ _____   ☐

10. Clock

3½ _____ ☐

4½ _____   ☐

5½ _____   ☐

	Response		*Age*	
		$3\frac{1}{2}$	$4\frac{1}{2}$	$5\frac{1}{2}$

11. Knife

$3\frac{1}{2}$	_____	☐		
$4\frac{1}{2}$	_____		☐	
$5\frac{1}{2}$	_____			☐

12. Washing machine

$3\frac{1}{2}$	_____	☐		
$4\frac{1}{2}$	_____		☐	
$5\frac{1}{2}$	_____			☐

13. Key

$3\frac{1}{2}$	_____	☐		
$4\frac{1}{2}$	_____		☐	
$5\frac{1}{2}$	_____			☐

14. Money

$3\frac{1}{2}$	_____	☐		
$4\frac{1}{2}$	_____		☐	
$5\frac{1}{2}$	_____			☐

(Continued on next page)

	Response	Age		
		3½	4½	5½

15. Telephone

3½	_____	☐		
4½	_____		☐	
5½	_____			☐

16. Window

3½	_____	☐		
4½	_____		☐	
5½	_____			☐

17. Calculator

3½	_____	☐		
4½	_____		☐	
5½	_____			☐

18. Umbrella

3½	_____	☐		
4½	_____		☐	
5½	_____			☐

GENERAL INFORMATION: SOLUTIONS TO PROBLEMS

WHAT SHOULD THEY DO?

Coming up with solutions to problems is more difficult than merely acquiring personal information. The simple problems presented below require the child to begin to draw on reasoning skills. In preschool children, the ability to reason is just emerging and generally involves little more than a concrete and familiar expression of the child's own experience.

Instructions: Tell the child, "I'm going to read about some children who have a problem. Let's see if you can help them." Write your child's responses on the lines, and then put the score in the boxes. (For general scoring instructions, see pages 45–49.) If your child misses three in a row, stop. Try again in a few months or at the next age level.

1. Billy had a lot of fun running and playing outside. When he came home, he felt hungry. What should Billy do so he won't be hungry?

Response	Age		
	3½	4½	5½
3½ _____	☐		
4½ _____		☐	
5½ _____			☐

2. Laura was playing outside in the snow when she realized how cold she felt. What should Laura do so she won't feel cold?

(Continued on next page)

	Response	Age		
		3½	4½	5½
3½	_____	☐		
4½	_____		☐	
5½	_____			☐

3. Jessica had had a very busy day. She had been up early in the morning, and it was getting late. She was so tired. What should Jessica do?

	Response	3½	4½	5½
3½	_____	☐		
4½	_____		☐	
5½	_____			☐

4. Michael was making mud pies in his yard when his mother called him to come inside for lunch. When he got inside, he looked at his hands and saw how dirty they were. What should Michael do so that he doesn't have dirty hands for lunch?

	Response	3½	4½	5½
3½	_____	☐		
4½	_____		☐	
5½	_____			☐

5. Deborah was playing in the family room. She wanted her doll. When she went to her room to get it, the room was dark and she couldn't see where her doll was. What should Deborah do?

Response	Age		
	3½	4½	5½
3½ _____	☐		
4½ _____		☐	
5½ _____			☐

6. Jim wanted to go next door to visit John. It was raining out. Jim didn't want to get wet. What should Jim do?

Response	3½	4½	5½
3½ _____	☐		
4½ _____		☐	
5½ _____			☐

7. Jennifer's cousin had come to visit from her home, which was far away. She did not know anything about Jennifer's town. When she went to buy some milk, she asked Jennifer where to go. Where did Jennifer tell her she could go to buy milk?

(Continued on next page)

Response	Age		
	3½	4½	5½
3½ _____	☐		
4½ _____		☐	
5½ _____			☐

(Child should name the right *kind* of store.)

GENERAL INFORMATION: FUNCTIONS OF PEOPLE

WHAT DO THEY DO?

As the child's awareness moves out from herself, she becomes aware of an ever-widening number of significant others. Of course, the first awareness is of Mommy and Daddy, brothers and sisters. But soon others, from the next-door neighbor to Bernie the mailman, are added to the list. An awareness of the people with whom the child comes into contact reflects a developing social and conceptual knowledge.

Instructions: For this game, show your child the pictures on the next few pages. For each picture, say, "Do you know what this person is?" If the answer is yes, say, "What does this person do?" If the child does not know, go on to the next item. Write your child's responses on the lines, and put the scores in the boxes. Score a plus if he knows more than one job function of a person. (For general scoring instructions, see pages 45–49.)

		Age		
		3½	4½	5½
3½	Person _____	☐		
	Job _____	☐		
4½	Person _____		☐	
	Job _____		☐	
5½	Person _____			☐
	Job _____			☐
3½	Person _____	☐		
	Job _____	☐		
4½	Person _____		☐	
	Job _____		☐	
5½	Person _____			☐
	Job _____			☐

(Continued on next page)

		Age		
		3½	4½	5½
3½	Person _____	☐		
	Job _____	☐		
4½	Person _____		☐	
	Job _____		☐	
5½	Person _____			☐
	Job _____			☐

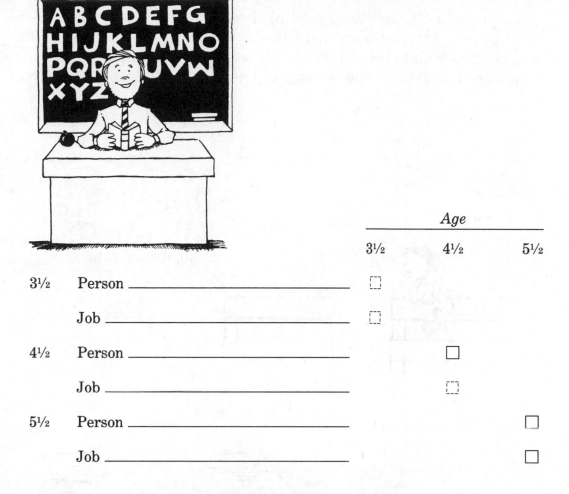

		Age	
	3½	4½	5½
3½ Person _____	☐		
Job _____	☐		
4½ Person _____		☐	
Job _____		☐	
5½ Person _____			☐
Job _____			☐

CONCEPTS

The child's ability to understand concepts that reflect the thinking underlying vocabulary development, the comprehension of people's roles and functions, and the logic needed for problem solving also extends to the development of the ability to conceptualize the abstract—relationships that do not refer to tangible things. For example, certain words and phrases, such as prepositions, deal with these relationship concepts. The use of such words reflects the child's developing ability to deal with problem solving and relationships through concepts.

(Continued on next page)

Instructions: The following pairs of pictures are presented with captions for one of the concepts. Read the caption under each pair and ask your child to point to the picture that shows what you have said. Scoring is on page 116. (For general scoring instructions, see pages 45–49.)

1. Socks on

2. No, it's not raining

3. Under the fence

4. In the house

5. Down the stairs

6. Stop

7. Above the clouds

8. From the store

9. Old shoes

10. Few fish

11. After the haircut

12. Full of water

(Continued on next page)

	Age		
	3½	4½	5½
1.	☐	☐	☐
2.	☐	☐	☐
3.	☐	☐	☐
4.	☐	☐	☐
5.	☐	☐	☐
6.	☐	☐	☐
7.	☐	☐	☐
8.	☐	☐	☐
9.	☐	☐	☐
10.	☐	☐	☐
11.	☐	☐	☐
12.	☐	☐	☐

GENERAL INFORMATION: NUMBER AWARENESS

HOW FAR CAN YOU COUNT?

Often, younger children can recite the numbers without having any idea of what the numbers mean. Knowing the names of the numbers does not mean the child can count objects. Nevertheless, this first number skill is often a source of great pride for a child.

Instructions: Say, "Let's see how far you can count. Start with number one, and keep counting." (For general scoring instructions, see pages 45–49.)

	Age		
	3½	4½	5½
1. Child counts to five	☐	☐	☐
2. Child counts to ten	☐	☐	☐
3. Child counts to fifteen	☐	☐	☐

BIGGER AND SMALLER

Before a child can understand numbers and counting, he must first develop some concepts of size and quantity. This game shows your child's emerging sense of what the measured world is all about.

Instructions: Show your child the pairs of drawings and ask him to point to the one that is larger, smaller, and so on, according to the directions with each set of pictures. (For general scoring instructions, see pages 45–49.)

	Age		
	3½	4½	5½
1. Point to the stick that is *larger*.	☐	☐	☐

	Age		
2. Point to the boy who is *bigger*.	☐	☐	☐

(Continued on next page)

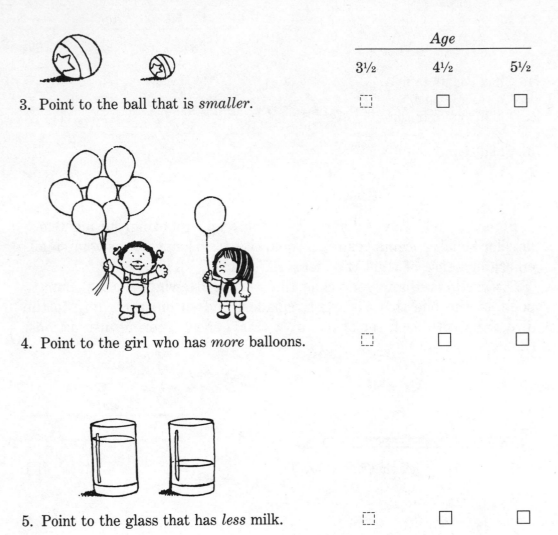

	Age		
	3½	4½	5½

3. Point to the ball that is *smaller*.

4. Point to the girl who has *more* balloons.

5. Point to the glass that has *less* milk.

SHOW ME YOUR FINGERS

Instructions: Ask your child to show you one finger, two fingers, then three fingers. Score the response correct if she holds up the right number of fingers on the first try. Don't worry if she has to use the fingers of the other hand for manipulating her fingers to get the right number. (For general scoring instructions, see pages 45–49.)

	Age		
	3½	4½	5½
1. "Show me one finger."	☐	☐	☐
2. "Show me two fingers."	☐	☐	☐
3. "Show me three fingers."	☐	☐	☐

HOW MANY BLOCKS?

Instructions: Ask your child, "Can you count the blocks in the pictures? Tell me how many there are." As he counts, note especially whether the child assigns one number to each block by touching it or pointing to it. (Sometimes a child will come up with the right number without actually counting the actual blocks. He may just recite the numbers and get lucky by happening to stop on the right number. Check the box only if the child maintains a one-to-one correspondence—one number for each block.) (For general scoring instructions, see pages 45–49.)

	Age		
	3½	4½	5½
1. Child counts correctly	☐	☐	☐
2. Child counts correctly	☐	☐	☐
3. Child counts correctly	☐	☐	☐

COUNT IN A CIRCLE

Instructions: Ask your child, "Can you count the blocks in the circle? Show me how you do it." Counting in a circle is a fairly tough task for most preschoolers for two reasons. First, it is difficult for them to remember where they started counting. Second, they may not yet understand that you can't count the same block twice. Therefore, they may count around the circle more than once before stopping at random. Do not point out to your child where he or she started, since that would side-step the point of the task. (For general scoring instructions, see pages 45–49.)

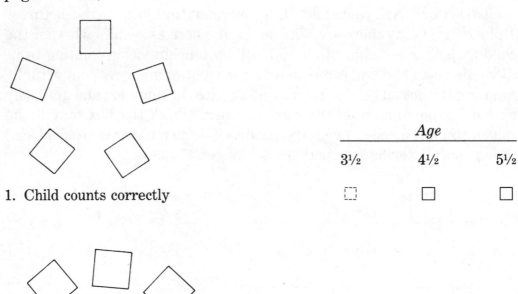

	Age		
	3½	4½	5½
1. Child counts correctly	⬚	☐	☐

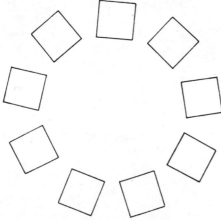

2. Child counts correctly	⬚	⬚	☐

NAME THAT NUMBER

Associating the name of a number with the symbol for the number is one of the early "symbolic" lessons a preschooler grasps.

Instructions: Say, "Look at all these numbers. Do you know them all? Tell me what each number is."

The first set of numbers contains easier symbols; those in the second set are harder for a preschooler to recognize and name. (For general scoring instructions, see pages 45–49.)

3 7 4 1 8

	Age		
	3½	4½	5½
1. Child gets three correct	☐	☐	☐
2. Child gets four correct	☐	☐	☐
3. Child gets five correct	☐	☐	☐

9 12 5 10 6

	3½	4½	5½
1. Child gets three correct	☐	☐	☐
2. Child gets four correct	☐	☐	☐
3. Child gets five correct	☐	☐	☐

WHAT TO DO WITH YOUR RESULTS

When looking at your results, it is important to keep the whole child in mind. Before drawing any firm conclusions, you will want to complete the observations in the other sections of the book in order to gain an overall picture. A problem in one area may not be a matter for concern; however, if a pattern of errors occurs in several or most of the areas covered by this book, you may want to consult professional help. Suggestions for how to proceed are indicated in each chapter.

Now that you've played the games and completed scoring the activities in this section, you have an idea of your child's general fund of information. Are there a lot of checks in solid boxes? Then your Emily knows what most children know—she is pretty much on target. Keep doing what you've been doing—or, if you'd like to help her increase her fund of information, try some of the suggestions presented under "What Can You Do?"

If there are one or two blank boxes, don't worry. The fact that each child is an individual means that not all children know all the same things. One or two misses do not indicate a problem. However, if there are three, four, or more blank boxes, Emily probably knows less about the world than most children her age. The games and suggestions under "What Can You Do?" may be of some help, or if you feel there is reason for concern, you may want to seek professional help to determine whether Emily is having a learning problem. The earlier such difficulties are detected, the better her chances are for full remediation.

And if there are a lot of pluses in boxes, this means Emily knows more than most of her peers. Chances are you're already playing games and doing activities similar to those we've outlined under "What Can You Do?" Good for you—because it's good for your child.

If you're at all concerned about Emily's general fund of information, check it out with the nursery-school or day-school teacher, if Emily goes to such a school. Remember to start with an open-ended question like "How's Emily doing?" to get the teacher's spontaneous response; then focus on the area you're concerned about with some specific questions. When you played the games in this section of the book, if Emily missed several questions about people's jobs, for instance, you might ask the teacher if Emily seems to be behind other children in this area. The teacher may feel that she really isn't so far behind the others as to give you cause to worry. (It's always possible that Emily was in a silly mood when you played the games with her and felt like pretending that she didn't know what a policeman does when actually she knows quite well.) The teacher *may* have a better idea of Emily's abilities in this area through observing her in school activities.

On the other hand, the teacher may agree with you that Emily does seem a little vague about the real world. This in itself need not be a matter for concern, but if it is combined with a lack of ability in some other area, you might want to do some more exploring.

It's unlikely that your pediatrician will know whether your child is behind in learning and general information, simply because the pediatrician probably doesn't see your child often enough to know how your child performs in this area. However, the doctor will be able to give you some suggestions as to whom you might consult.

When you combine the results from this section with the results from the other sections of the book, you may want to receive further information or help from some of the sources discussed below and in subsequent chapters.

1. *A child study team.* Child study teams are composed of a number of specialists that may differ from place to place, depending on the setting. A hospital's team would probably be more medically oriented than a university psychology department's team. A rehabilitation center's team would include physical and/or occupational therapists, while a psychology center's team might not.

   Some of the specialists you might find on a child study team are a psychologist, a speech and language therapist, a nurse, a pediatric neurologist, a physical therapist, an occupational therapist (or a PT/OT, responsible for both types of therapy), a social worker, and a child psychologist.

   Since different teams are made of different specialists, you will need to find one whose members are trained in those areas where your child needs help. If you and your pediatrician suspect a motor-skills problem, the team that screens your child must include a pediatric neurologist to check for nerve function. Your pediatrician will be able to help you find the team that is right for your child's needs.

2. *A child guidance clinic.* Most communities fund such a clinic at reduced fees. It is worth noting that a child guidance clinic may have a waiting list, so you may not be able to have the evaluation performed immediately.

3. *A child psychologist.* Psychologists in private practice are more expensive than clinics, but there will probably be no waiting list. Not all persons in private practice are licensed or certified. Be sure to check.
4. *Your public school's preschool evaluation program.*
5. *Child Find.* For an explanation of this program, see page 36.

Remember to check your major medical insurance policy. Evaluation and treatment by some or all of these professionals may or may not be covered by it.

If you do decide to see a specialist, he or she will probably recommend a specific course of action to help your child. One possibility the specialist may suggest is a preschool or nursery-school program, or a continuation of such a program if Emily is already in one. (If your child is approaching kindergarten age, the specialist may recommend that she get an extra year of nursery school under her belt before going on to the challenge of public school.) Another possibility is the repeating of kindergarten. (Don't look on this as a failure for you or Emily. The starting time at which children are ready for reading and writing varies from child to child. It's not uncommon to discover that a particular child needs more growing time before the plunge into first grade.)

It's worth noting here that at this early age, repeating a year usually doesn't bother a child. If Emily has to stay back in third or fourth grade, *then* she is likely to be upset. That's another reason to repeat kindergarten if events call for it.

However, the child who is a slow learner may not benefit from repeating a year; he or she will continue to follow a slow-learning pattern the second time, just as he or she did the first. These children may require special programs or classes or a special school where their special needs can be met in an individualized way.

WHAT CAN YOU DO?

Whether Emily scores high or low on our activities, there are lots of things you can do to help her develop learning skills and increase her fund of general information.

For a start, you can foster the idea that it's fun to learn new things. Express appreciation when Emily comes to you with new discoveries, and treat her questions seriously. You don't have to turn every answer into a lecture, but you can take advantage of her interest to encourage learning.

When Alison asks "How come there are so many worms on the sidewalk today?" her father explains that it's because it rained last night, and rain brings the worms out of the ground. But not leaving it at that, he goes over to where his daughter is squatting down, and he looks at the worm with her. "See that smooth band around the middle? The worm's eggs are in there," he explains. Alison is fascinated. "Tommy has a book about worms," her father says. "Why don't you ask him to read parts of it to you?" By the end of the morning, Alison knows more about worms than anyone else in her family.

Jared asks his mother the same question: "How come there are so many worms out today?" His mother, busy thumbing through the bills the mailman has just brought, takes the easy way out. "I don't know, honey," she murmurs. Jared is left wondering, and with no way to satisfy his curiosity. He also gets the idea that it really doesn't matter very much why the worms are out, so it's not worth trying to find out.

Besides taking Emily's questions seriously, you can play information games as a family activity. Play "Twenty Questions" when you're out in the car. The leader thinks of an object and tells the other players whether it's animal, vegetable, or mineral. The players then can ask twenty questions to help them guess the object. The questions have to be the kind that can be answered with yes or no. Whoever guesses the object first gets to be leader for the next game. Of course, for younger children, the game should be kept as simple as possible, but older children will enjoy the challenge of more difficult objects.

Play the "Whose House Is This?" game. Describe a home, and let Emily guess who lives there. For instance: "It's made of twigs and grass, lined with feathers, and it's high up in a tree." (A bird's nest.)

Encourage an interest in nature by observing what's around you when you go for a walk. Whether you live in the woods or in the city, there's a lot to see and learn about, and your child will be full of questions. If you don't know the answers, say "I don't know—let's look it up." You can go to the library and take out books on the subject, letting your child help you choose.

You can help Emily to learn about cause-and-effect by drawing her attention to the things that happen around the house. "Look! When I put a drop of soap in the greasy water, all the grease zips away to the edge of the pan!" You don't have to go into an explanation of why this happens unless you feel Emily is capable of understanding it. Just drawing her attention to the wonder of the event is a good start. When she is older, you can encourage investigation into the causes.

And of course, read to her. Read nursery rhymes, fairy tales, fiction, and nonfiction. Read all different kinds of books. It's just as important for a four-year-old to know about Mother Goose as it is to know about animals on the farm; poetry is just as important as prose.

Play different kinds of music, from children's songs to Tchaikovsky. Expose Emily to as many experiences as you can, and let her develop her own tastes and preferences. A child who has never been exposed to the Beatles is missing something, just as a child who has never heard the "1812" Overture is missing something. (By the way, the "1812" Overture, with its bells and cannons, is a sure child-pleaser and a terrific way to introduce Emily to classical music.)

There's a fringe benefit to helping your child notice and wonder the world around us: You'll find that your own wonder and delight in the world are renewed as you see it through her eyes.

·7·

Language
Development

At the age of one day, there's not much difference between David and Susie—except that David is a human baby and Susie is a chimpanzee. They're both helpless, and their mothers have to do everything for them. About all they can do is cry.

Within a month, Susie has a distinct edge over David. She can get around by herself, and she can communicate everything she'll ever need to as well as she'll ever be able to. If she wants food, she knows how to ask for it. If she's scared or mad, she knows how to express her feeling.

Meanwhile, back in the nursery, David at one month is still barely able to lift his head. Only his mother can distinguish between his hungry cry and his wet-diapers cry. Observing the two infants, a visitor from outer space would have no trouble deciding which is the more intelligent species.

Two years later, Susie is swinging through the trees while David is still tottering. He can't see as far as she can, he can't hear as keenly, and he can't smell as well. But, boy, *can he talk*! And that's the unique ability that gives humans capabilities far beyond other living things: we have a language, and we know how to use it.

Language is closely allied to intelligence because it is the tool most commonly used to express intelligence. In fact, the bond between the two is so close that some people mistakenly equate them. Early immigration officials, for instance, tended to think that immigrants were unintelligent because the newcomers couldn't answer the simplest questions, spoken in the clearest, slowest *English*!

Your child's language skills are probably the most important single handle for getting a grip on who and where he or she is. What David talks about tells you what's going on inside. If he is significantly behind other children of the same age in vocabulary and the ability to express ideas and opinions, this may be an indication of problems that you will want to discuss with qualified professionals. And even if there is no underlying problem, you may want to consider giving serious attention to your child's language difficulties for one simple reason: other people's perception of his intelligence is colored by the skill with which he communicates. If David has a speech problem—a stutter, for instance—other people may perceive him as being less intelligent than he is. They may then treat him as a less intelligent person, with the conceivable result that, perpetuating the vicious circle, he may turn out to be less intelligent than he might have been.

Language is important for another reason: the language a child learns influences the problems he can tackle. Take, as two extreme examples, Eskimos and Navajos.

The Eskimo language has dozens of words for snow, each reflecting a different condition, a different type of snow. Using these words, which reflect an important reality for Eskimos, an Eskimo child can make fine distinctions and differentiations between one type of snow and another. This is an important skill for Eskimos, because their travel, their food, sometimes even their shelter can all depend on the ability to make this distinction. David, on the other hand, only needs to know that there's cold white stuff on the ground, and he'd better wear boots and a warm coat. One or two words are all he needs to talk about snow.

Navajos have a single word that deals with the concept of space-time. English does not have such a word—in fact, it is difficult for people who are raised speaking English to comprehend that space and time are merely different aspects of the same basic concept. Navajos, though, are quick to understand that aspect of Einsteinian relativity, because both their language and their philosophy include the concept.

On a more down-to-earth, day-to-day basis, the vocabulary and language skills your child picks up will affect his ability to learn. Children who are brought up in what we call an "expanded language environment" perform a great deal better on IQ tests, reading tests, and school achievement tests than do children whose language environment is impoverished.

Out for a walk with his mother, Mark points and asks, "What's that?" "A dog," says his mother, who is busy with her own thoughts. And that's that. When David spies the same dog and asks the same question, his mother says, "That's a dalmatian. Boy, he's just covered with little round black spots, isn't he?" David agrees, and the conversation goes on to cover the fact that many firehouses used to have this kind of dog for a mascot. "What's a mascot?" David asks, and the conversation then reaches out to take in the time David went to the football game and saw the man dressed up as a chicken. By the time they have gone around the block, David's vocabulary has been made richer and more interesting. He has found that there is more than one word for a dog, and in the process he has begun to grasp that he can do more with language than simply label things.

Meanwhile, Mark is being less well equipped. When he is older—in kindergarten and first grade, for example—when he has trouble making people understand his ideas, he may give up. He only knows one or two ways to communicate a concept, so although the ideas may be there, he can't bring them forth for other people to see and share.

It is in school that language difficulties cause the most frustration. We're not talking about small problems—a lisp, or the tendency to say "lellow" instead of "yellow," for instance. These are minor glitches; they don't seriously interfere with communication, and most children eventually outgrow them. But a child who consistently has trouble finding the right words may have a problem; the child who consistently gets his word order mixed up may be on the road to difficulties that will plague him throughout the school years and beyond.

Granted, a parent may not be able to distinguish between a child who is simply having temporary difficulties with language and one who is heading for serious trouble. If you have any doubt at all as to whether your child needs help with language skills, there are professionals who can help you make that determination and tell you how to get the help you need.

Research has shown that there are two likely times for a child to begin reading. Early readers—generally the verbally gifted children—begin at four and a half or five, with encouragement from their parents. Other children begin to acquire this skill at six or six and a half. Between these two times, there is a gap during which children less often begin learning to read. Apparently there's too much else going on during the year between five and six; the child doesn't have much attention to spare for this important skill. If your child happens to be an early reader, that's great! But if Marie or Danny doesn't pick it up at the age of five, you might as well settle back and wait out the next year without worrying. When they're ready, probably around six, they'll learn to read without much trouble.

Like all the other skills a child acquires, language skills develop in an outward-moving way. They begin very close to home, and they wander further afield as the child matures.

Young David, at the age of two, is still learning basic, get-through-the-day vocabulary. Words relating to his personal wants and needs are high on his list: *Mommy, Daddy, cookie, drink, no.* A two-year-old's vocabulary is very fundamental. But as he gets older, he begins to talk about experiences less directly related to himself. He talks about his friends, his family, his teachers—and he can discuss things going on in the world around him in a fairly abstract way.

It's worth noting here that when we say "the world around him," we mean that fairly literally. David may, when he is five, begin to talk about war. But what he is talking about is the war *he himself* has experienced—through watching the six-o'clock news. He has no actual experience of war, even though it is part of his vocabulary. This is a prime example of the effect of TV on our kids: it has vastly widened their superficial experiences without giving them real learning experiences. TV enables little David to label war but not to understand it.

At two and a half, David talks to himself constantly while he plays. He's talking about the here-and-now, about what he's working on and what he's thinking about. He has learned to use the pronouns *I, me,* and *you*; no longer does he say "David go bye-bye, too!" Now it's "I go with you." (Only it's "wiv you.")

At this age, most of his conversations are with adults. These conversations are concerned with getting, giving, and learning about his world. He's full of "what" and "where" questions. "Where's Mickey?" When told that his brother Mickey is in his room: "What did he did?" (Grammar is far from perfect at this age.) He can speak in clusters of as many as ten words: "What's that? I want that hat. Give it to me." But in his eagerness to get the words out, he sometimes stutters.

By the time he's three, he can string six words together in a sentence, and it's likely to be a question: what, where, or who? His speech is pretty clear—he has mastered that tricky *th* sound that used to give him trouble. But he still tends to lisp, a problem that won't fade away until he's almost five.

At three, David's inflection is charming. His mother loves to stand in the next room and listen to him talk. She can't hear the words, but she loves the sound of his little voice going up and down, sounding so adult and reasonable. He has a vocabulary of nine hundred words, and he talks to himself constantly, in an ongoing monologue that includes a great deal of make-believe as well as descriptions of what's going on around him.

When he reaches the age of four, David is beginning to understand that words are tools. If you ask him what a word in his vocabulary means, chances are he will be able to tell you. This is an important step—it means he can think of more than one way of saying some things. His knowledge and understanding of language are growing fast now. His vocabulary has increased to over fifteen hundred words, and his parents are willing to testify that he uses them all, every day, over and over and over!

He is using his words differently now—not just to get, give, and learn, but to socialize, to communicate with his family and his friends. This skill grows along with his increased tendency toward cooperative play: "Let's make mud pies. I'll get the water."

At five, David's vocabulary includes over two thousand words. He likes words—he likes to know what they mean. He asks for the meaning of abstract words and demonstrates logical reasoning. "I know why skunks smell pewie," he explains to his father. "They sneeze out of their tails!"

David knows that a joke is when one person says something and the other people laugh. So: "Want to hear a joke? Dirty socks!" he says, and he waits for the laugh. As far as he's concerned, labeling this remark "joke" is enough to draw a laugh. He doesn't quite understand what would make the remark funny.

His sense of formal language structure is still faulty, but he does know that language has some rules. For instance, he understands that you add *s* to a word if you're talking about more than one. Applying that rule, he comes up with this sentence: "Mayonnaise don't taste very good by themselves, do they?" (He hears the *s* at the end of *mayonnaise* and assumes that it indicates the plural form of "mayonnay.")

It is at this age that David composes his first poem.

There's the little duck.
It won't eat you up.
You can touch it with your hand,
Then you can come to the land.

It doesn't make a whole lot of sense, but it rhymes and it scans. He is very proud of himself for creating it—and he should be.

When he's six, David will at last be able to tell his parents what happened in the last rerun of "Little House on the Prairie"—in the correct sequence. No more backtracking to fill in vital information that he forgot.

Now he can even tell reasonably good jokes. They're not new jokes ("What's black and white and red all over?" is at least twenty-five years old to our certain knowledge), but at least they make sense and he understands why they're funny.

He's come a long way from "David go bye-bye, too"! Now he's ready to use his language skills in reading, thinking, and learning more about the world. Your child, too, is expanding vocabulary and language skills. To watch these skills develop over the months, play the word games and activities we've suggested below.

Language Measures

EXPRESSIVE VOCABULARY

Word knowledge as reflected in vocabulary is a key indicator of a child's use of the human ability to conceptualize, record, and deal with one's world and experience. Language is built on the basic blocks of vocabulary. The words a child actually uses reflect his active command of daily living.

For starters, inventory your child's vocabulary. For one week, write down each different word your child uses. This will give you an opportunity to assess the number of words your child uses spontaneously. While you're at it, make a note of any mispronunciations or other difficulties in articulation. Keep the list in the file you're compiling for your child.

RECEPTIVE / EXPRESSIVE VOCABULARY

WHAT DO YOU SEE?

Instructions: Say, "I'll point to some pictures—you tell me what each picture shows."

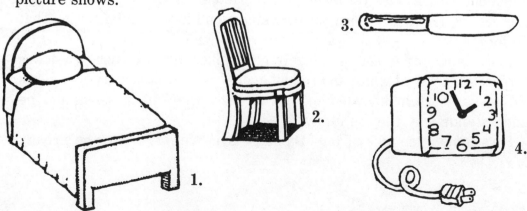

1.

2.

3.

4.

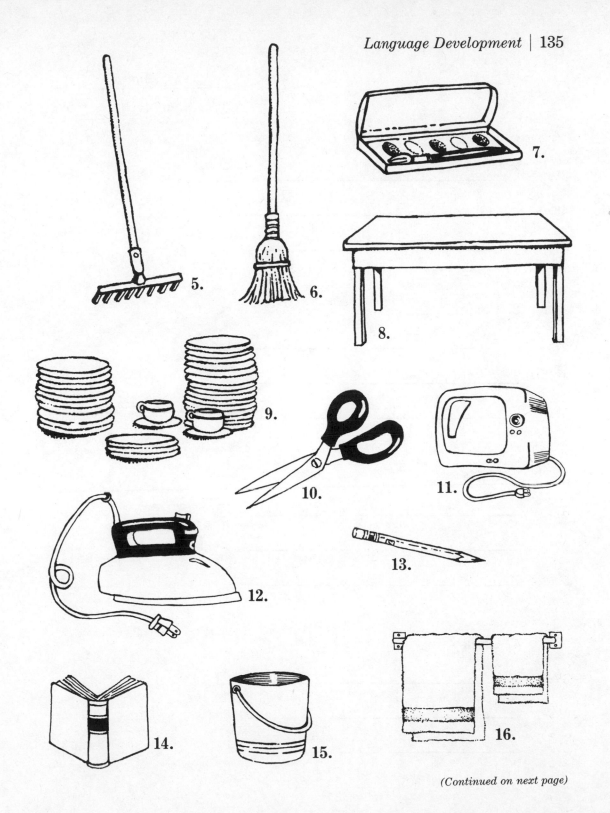

5.

6.

7.

8.

9.

10.

11.

12.

13.

14.

15.

16.

(Continued on next page)

	Age		
	3½	4½	5½

1. Bed

3½	_____	☐		
4½	_____		☐	
5½	_____			☐

2. Chair

3½	_____	☐		
4½	_____		☐	
5½	_____			☐

3. Knife

3½	_____	☐		
4½	_____		☐	
5½	_____			☐

4. Clock

3½	_____	☐		
4½	_____		☐	
5½	_____			☐

	Age		
	3½	4½	5½

5. Rake

3½	_____	☐		
4½	_____		☐	
5½	_____			☐

6. Broom

3½	_____	☐		
4½	_____		☐	
5½	_____			☐

7. Paints

3½	_____	☐		
4½	_____		☐	
5½	_____			☐

8. Table

3½	_____	☐		
4½	_____		☐	
5½	_____			☐

(Continued on next page)

	Age		
	3½	4½	5½

9. Dishes

3½	_____	☐		
4½	_____		☐	
5½	_____			☐

10. Scissors

3½	_____	☐		
4½	_____		☐	
5½	_____			☐

11. TV

3½	_____	☐		
4½	_____		☐	
5½	_____			☐

12. Iron

3½	_____	☐		
4½	_____		☐	
5½	_____			☐

	Age		
	3½	4½	5½

13. Pencil

3½ _____ ☐

4½ _____   ☐

5½ _____   ☐

14. Book

3½ _____ ☐

4½ _____   ☐

5½ _____   ☐

15. Pail

3½ _____ ☐

4½ _____   ☐

5½ _____   ☐

16. Towels

3½ _____ ☐

4½ _____   ☐

5½ _____   ☐

WHAT IS IT?

One of the first uses of words is to attach a word label to objects in the child's world. Recognizing the word and expressing its meaning constitute the full cycle of language as a tool.

Instructions: Tell your child you're going to say some words. Say, "If you know what the word means, what it is, or what it does, tell me." Write the child's response on the line. Most younger children define a word by saying what he or she would do with the object.

If your child can give a correct response, put the score in the box after the word. (For general scoring instructions, see pages 45–49.)

	Response	*Age*		
		3½	4½	5½
1. Orange				
3½	_____	☐		
4½	_____		☐	
5½	_____			☐
2. Ball				
3½	_____	☐		
4½	_____		☐	
5½	_____			☐
3. Block				
3½	_____	☐		
4½	_____		☐	
5½	_____			☐

Response	*Age*		
	$3\frac{1}{2}$	$4\frac{1}{2}$	$5\frac{1}{2}$

4. Table

$3\frac{1}{2}$ _____ ☐

$4\frac{1}{2}$ _____   ☐

$5\frac{1}{2}$ _____   ☐

5. Key

$3\frac{1}{2}$ _____ ☐

$4\frac{1}{2}$ _____   ☐

$5\frac{1}{2}$ _____   ☐

6. Horn

$3\frac{1}{2}$ _____ ☐

$4\frac{1}{2}$ _____   ☐

$5\frac{1}{2}$ _____   ☐

7. Bicycle

$3\frac{1}{2}$ _____ ☐

$4\frac{1}{2}$ _____   ☐

$5\frac{1}{2}$ _____   ☐

(Continued on next page)

	Response	*Age*		
		3½	4½	5½

8. Moon

3½	_____	☐		
4½	_____		☐	
5½	_____			☐

9. Juggle

3½	_____	☐		
4½	_____		☐	
5½	_____			☐

10. Window

3½	_____	☐		
4½	_____		☐	
5½	_____			☐

11. Robin

3½	_____	☐		
4½	_____		☐	
5½	_____			☐

Response	Age		
	3½	4½	5½

12. Closet

3½ _____ ☐

4½ _____   ☐

5½ _____   ☐

13. Iron

3½ _____ ☐

4½ _____   ☐

5½ _____   ☐

14. Thermometer

3½ _____ ☐

4½ _____   ☐

5½ _____   ☐

WHAT ARE THEY DOING?

The ability to express actions rather than simply label objects is a step forward in each child's language development. The pictures on the next page can help you gauge your child's development of this skill.

Instructions: Say, "I'll show you some pictures. You tell me what the people are doing in each one."

1.

2.

3.

4.

5.

6.

7.

8.

9.

10.

11.

	Age		
	3½	4½	5½

1. Eating

3½ _____ ☐

4½ _____   ☐

5½ _____   ☐

2. Washing face

3½ _____ ☐

4½ _____   ☐

5½ _____   ☐

3. Brushing teeth

3½ _____ ☐

4½ _____   ☐

5½ _____   ☐

4. Dancing

3½ _____ ☐

4½ _____   ☐

5½ _____   ☐

(Continued on next page)

	Age		
	3½	4½	5½

5. Building

3½	☐		
4½		☐	
5½			☐

6. Jumping

3½	☐		
4½		☐	
5½			☐

7. Swinging

3½	☐		
4½		☐	
5½			☐

8. Drawing

3½	☐		
4½		☐	
5½			☐

		Age	
	3½	4½	5½

9. Reading

3½	_____	☐		
4½	_____		☐	
5½	_____			☐

10. Writing

3½	_____	☐		
4½	_____		☐	
5½	_____			☐

11. Crawling

3½	_____	☐		
4½	_____		☐	
5½	_____			☐

RECEPTIVE LANGUAGE

TELL ME A STORY

A great deal of information comes to children in the form of language. How well they receive and recall that information is an important part of their language ability.

Instructions: Say, "I'm going to tell you a story, and then I want you to tell me the same story." Read the stories given here, and have your child try to tell the story back to you. Write down *whatever* your child says, even if it seems unrelated to the story. Then score your child's version of the story. We're not looking for memorization, necessarily— if your child has the gist of the story, that will be fine.

FLUFFY THE KITTY

Fluffy was a kitty. She had a mother. She had two brothers. Fluffy liked milk.

	Age		
	3½	4½	5½
3½ _____	☐		
_____			
_____			
(If child remembers two or three facts, score a check. If child remembers all four facts, score a plus.)			
4½ _____		☐	
_____			
_____			
(If child remembers all four facts, score a check. If child repeats story verbatim, score a plus.)			
5½ _____			☐
_____			
_____			
(If child repeats story verbatim, score a check.)			

JIMMY GOES TO THE CIRCUS

Jimmy went to the circus. He saw elephants. He saw some funny clowns. He saw a monkey riding a horse. He liked the tigers best.

		Age		
		3½	4½	5½
3½	_____	☐		

(If child remembers two or three facts, score a check. If child remembers four or five facts, score a plus.)

4½	_____		☐	

(If child remembers four or five facts, score a check. If child repeats story verbatim, score a plus.)

5½	_____			☐

(If child repeats story verbatim, score a check.)

RUNAWAY BROWNIE

Jane had a pony. The pony's name was Brownie. Brownie jumped over a fence. He ran away. He was gone all day. But he got lonely and came home. Jane was glad to see him.

(Continued on next page)

	Age		
	3½	4½	5½
3½	☐		

(If child remembers two or three facts, score a check. If child remembers four or more facts, score a plus.)

4½		☐	

(If child remembers four or five facts, score a check. If child remembers six or more facts, score a plus.)

5½			☐

(If child remembers six to eight facts, score a check. If child repeats story verbatim, score a plus.)

PICTURE LANGUAGE

WHAT'S HAPPENING HERE?

We can learn something about the way kids look at the world from the way they look at pictures. At first, looking at a picture, they'll see only separate, unrelated items: a table, a chair, a lady, a boy, a glass, a baseball mitt. At a later stage, they'll see things in relationship to each other: The lady is the mother, giving the boy water. Finally, they'll begin to make inferences about what happened before and after the scene: The mother got the water from the kitchen, and when the boy is through drinking, he's going to play baseball.

Instructions: Show your child the picture. Say, "Look at this picture. Tell me a story about the picture. Tell me what is happening now, what happened before, and what's going to happen next." Write the child's response on the lines and put the appropriate score in the box. (For general scoring instructions, see pages 45–49.)

(Continued on next page)

	Age		
	3½	4½	5½
3½ _____	☐		
_____			
(If child names two objects and one action, score a check. If child names more than two objects and one action, score a plus.)			
4½ _____		☐	
_____			
(If child names four objects and several actions, score a check. If child includes actions in past or future, score a plus.)			
5½ _____			☐
_____			
(If child names five or six objects and several actions, score a check. If child names many objects and actions and includes both past and future, score a plus.)			

FOLLOWING INSTRUCTIONS

SIMON SAYS

As a child matures, she is increasingly able to remember a sequence of instructions in the correct order. This game can help you gain an understanding of your child's ability to correctly remember a sequence of actions—a skill that is necessary in school in order to follow directions.

Instructions: Say, "Let's play Simon Says. I'll tell you what Simon says to do, and then you do it." (You can give a demonstration to help your child understand how the game works.) This game traditionally involves tricking people into doing things Simon does *not* say to do. For the purpose of this evaluation, you don't want to trick your child; "Simon" should "say" each of the commands.

If your child correctly performs the sequence, put a check in the box. (For general scoring instructions, see pages 45–49.)

	Age		
	3½	4½	5½
1. One-step instructions: "Put the block on the chair."	☐	☐	☐
2. Two-step instructions: "Take the block off the table and go sit on the sofa."	☐	☐	☐
3. Three-step instructions: "Close the door, turn on the light, and open the book."	☐	☐	☐
4. Four-step instructions: "Turn off the light, close the door, bring me the book, and give me a kiss!"	☐	☐	☐

VOCABULARY: BODY PARTS

SIMON SAYS AGAIN

Does your child have the language needed to label the parts of his body? This game can help you to find out. It can also help you to judge your child's awareness of himself as he locates the various parts of his body.

Instructions: Say, "Let's play Simon Says again." Explain the rules of the game again, if need be: "I'll tell you what Simon says to do, and then you see if you can do it." Again, you can give one demonstration, and again, your object is not to trick your child into doing what Simon does not say to do; all of your commands should be prefaced with "Simon says." The following list names the body parts that children are expected to recognize between the ages of three and five. Simply say, "Simon says 'Touch your head' (or chest or elbow)" for each item on this list. If your child can identify the body part, score a check. (For general scoring instructions, see pages 45–49.)

	Age		
	3½	4½	5½
1. Head	☐	☐	☐
2. Hand	☐	☐	☐
3. Arm	☐	☐	☐
4. Foot	☐	☐	☐
5. Knee	☐	☐	☐
6. Nose	☐	☐	☐
7. Ear	☐	☐	☐
8. Leg	☐	☐	☐
9. Elbow	☐	☐	☐
10. Wrist	☐	☐	☐
11. Toes	☐	☐	☐
12. Fingers	☐	☐	☐
13. Mouth	☐	☐	☐
14. Eyes	☐	☐	☐

DISCRIMINATION: COLOR

SCAVENGER COLOR-HUNT

The concept of color is one of the easiest—and earliest—for a young child to grasp because he can see the difference between red and yellow without having to think about it or to label the colors. In order to discern which two colors are the same, the child must also be able to tell which colors are different. This game can help you to see how well your child differentiates things that are not alike and associates things that are the same.

Instructions: For this game, you'll need a variety of colored items. A box of crayons offers a good choice of colors. Select one crayon, show it to your child, and say, "Find something in this room that's the same color as this crayon." (It might be wise to check ahead of time and make sure that there is something in the room to match every color you plan to use.) Good colors for this game are red, blue, green, yellow, orange, purple, black, and brown. Note that it is not necessary for the child to *identify* the colors—simply to *match* them. (For general scoring instructions, see pages 45–49.)

	Age		
	3½	4½	5½
1. Child matches two colors	☐	☐	☐
2. Child matches four colors	☐	☐	☐
3. Child matches all eight colors	☐	☐	☐

WHAT TO DO WITH YOUR RESULTS

Now that you've played the games in this chapter, you have an idea of where your child stands in the area of language and vocabulary. If there are a lot of pluses, that's great! Your child is doing better than most kids in verbal matters.

If your child's score included few empty boxes and few pluses but a lot of checks, then he or she is keeping up with most of the children in the same age group.

If there are a lot of empty boxes, your child may not be doing as well verbally as other children of the same age. This in itself may not be a matter for concern—although difficulties in language acquisition do tend to spill over into other areas, particularly when it's time for public school. However, if language difficulties are combined with difficulties in other areas, consultation with specialists is probably indicated.

The first place to check is the nursery school. Remember to start by asking the teacher a general "How is Chris doing?" type of question. Listen for an answer that indicates that the teacher is hesitating or is looking for ways to tell you that there are problems. If the teacher's response is too general, zero in with specific questions on the areas you're concerned about. Don't, however, ask, "Is he as verbal as other kids in the class?" Teachers are sensitive to the pitfalls of comparing one child to another or to all the others, so you may not get the information you're looking for. Instead, ask, "Does he speak out in class? Does he volunteer to answer questions? When he tells you a story, does it make sense to you?" To these questions, a good teacher can give you helpful responses in terms of what is expected of most children at this age. For instance, the teacher might say, "I can understand his stories as well as one *ever* understands a story told by a preschooler. Very few toddlers can tell a connected story!"

It happens fairly often that a child's articulation—ability to form speech sounds—is so imperfect that only the parents can understand it. If other people seem to have trouble understanding Chris, you might want to ask if the teacher has had the same problem. If the teacher feels that there is no cause for concern, that Chris's articulation is more or less average for his age, the problem is probably not a lasting one.

However, if, when you leave the nursery-school teacher, you're convinced that Chris might have a problem in verbal skills or articulation, the next person to go to is the pediatrician.

The pediatrician is not likely to have a good grip on Chris's vocabulary abilities simply because the doctor doesn't see Chris more than once or twice a year. However, he or she can help to determine whether Chris has a physical problem that might be causing articulation difficulties; if there are articulation problems, the pediatrician should be able to send you to the right specialist.

(It's important to remember that most toddlers have imperfect speech. Katie has a lisp; Peter substitutes *v* for *th*—almost any child will have at least one quirk of pronunciation. Usually these idiosyncrasies disappear by themselves. But some of them don't. And it usually takes a specialist to tell the difference between a long-term problem and a temporary one.)

Your pediatrician will probably do a quick test to check Chris's hearing. (As Jason Evans's parents discovered, when a child's hearing is not sharp, he doesn't hear the words clearly and therefore can't pronounce them correctly.) If the pediatrician suspects hearing problems, he or she will probably recommend a hearing specialist, who will do an in-depth evaluation of Chris's hearing.

If Chris's speech problem seems to call for further evaluation, you will probably be sent to a speech and language therapist. It's important for you to know whether the specialist deals only with articulation problems or is trained to deal with all aspects of language development.

Rehabilitation centers sometimes offer language evaluation facilities, and of course your public school's preschool evaluation team will also be able to help you. In particular, if Chris is reaching kindergarten age, your public school will routinely check his speech and hearing as part of their regular screening. They may even catch problems before you become aware of them. But if you become concerned when Chris is still too young for kindergarten, you can still call on your public school system for help. They can screen children as young as two years of age, and they will be more than happy to do so. They know that language is one of the areas in which problems can be detected—and often successfully dealt with—at an early age.

Because language problems can sometimes be rooted in psychological problems, part of the language screening will probably be a psychological evaluation performed by a child psychologist.

As a rule, language difficulties can be caused by any of three factors. The first is an environment that is not sufficiently language-stimulating. Jennie, whose parents tend to speak briefly, if at all, will not have the same ease with the language as her friend Mark, whose parents are talkative and encourage Mark to talk, too.

The second factor that can cause language problems is specific language disorders. These include developmental language delays, brain damage caused by illness or injury, and congenital birth defects, such as cleft palate.

The third factor that can cause language problems is emotional. Emotional problems can range from mild—simple shyness, for instance—to the very severe: autism and childhood schizophrenia, for example. (In fact, lack of language development or unusual language development is quite common in both of these illnesses.)

If evaluation establishes that Chris does have a language problem, it is possible that the therapist will recommend individual therapy. Usually, however, one-on-one therapy is recommended for relatively few preschoolers. As a rule, language therapists prefer to wait until the child's language has developed a little more fully so that they will have a better understanding of the child's particular patterns and problems.

There are preschool language programs associated with most public schools. (In fact, the Head Start program was designed largely to help children from disadvantaged environments to build language skills so they could keep up when they reached public school.)

WHAT CAN YOU DO?

There's a lot you can do to help increase Chris's language abilities, whether he is above or below normal in this area.

First, remember that language is a puzzle with many pieces. It involves listening, paying attention, hearing, remembering, and expression. You can provide opportunities for Chris in all of these areas.

The most important thing you can do is to talk to him and to other members of your family. Expand on simple information. Explain what you are doing and why: "Let's put our coats on before we go out because it's cold out there and we don't want to freeze." "Now I need to sift the flour to get all the lumps out. We don't want lumps in our cake, do we?" If you use words easily, your child will, too. And if you don't use words easily—if language skills are difficult for you—don't give up. Practice! You can develop your own skills while helping your child improve his.

Children are so imitative—they use the words they hear being used. They may not understand them at first, but they soon will. Four-year-old Alison, who is in the process of losing an argument with her friend Matt, squelches him with this sentence: "*That's* a different situation!" She's heard her father say that, though she doesn't know what it means. Neither does Matt—but he's impressed, and he stops trying to argue with her.

The next most important thing you can do for Chris is something that will take self-discipline on your part: Listen. Pay attention. When he comes home from school and starts telling you a long, confused story about what happened on the playground, be patient. Keep listening— really listening. Ask questions to help him get his story straight, but don't be impatient. Remember that at this age, most children can't tell a story in consecutive order. There will be a great deal of backtracking and "Oh, I forgot to say . . ." He'll start a sentence, get hung up on one word, and go back to the beginning of the sentence—over and over in a cycle of repetition: "There was a—There was a—There was a—" Hang in there. Don't try to finish his sentence for him. He'll make it by himself. And don't cut him off or tune him out. If you do, you're sending him a message: "You're boring me, and it's not worth my while to listen to you." Who could develop language ability faced with that kind of reception?

Building Language Skills

Read to your child. This is one of the most important things you can do to increase verbal skills. Let Chris hear words the way other people use them. Reading to children—especially poetry—gives them a feel for the rhythm and flow of language. This can be helpful in improving language skills and in helping the child develop an affection for words.

Read the same books over and over. (Just be sure they are books you enjoy yourself. It's a mistake to feel that you have to force yourself to read books you dislike or that bore you. There are plenty of excellent children's books out there that parents can enjoy. The books about Frances the badger, by Russell and Lillian Hoban, for instance, give adults as much pleasure as they give children.) Reading the same book until the child has it memorized can be very helpful in building facility with language. You'll find Chris using expressions from his favorite books. Katie, whenever something turns out just right, uses this expression: "And it was still hot!" Readers of Maurice Sendak's *Where the Wild Things Are* will recognize that line as the conclusion to Max's adventure, when he returns home to find his dinner waiting for him.

If Chris seems to have trouble paying attention as you read, start by explaining briefly what the story is about. "This is about some ducks who wanted to find a safe place to lay their eggs, and how they raised their babies and then took them to live right in the middle of the big city!" This can arouse his interest and help him to pay attention to the whole thing.

Play word games—especially when you're traveling in the car. This has a double advantage: it improves Chris's vocabulary, and it keeps him entertained. Try this one to improve listening skills: You say a short sentence and ask Chris to say it back. You can make the sentences silly: "Alison put the cat on her head" or "Cars have pretty wings." This can improve listening skills and give you a chance to check his hearing at the same time. If he consistently provides incorrect words that sound like the one you used—"Alison put the cat on her bed," for instance— you might suspect a hearing problem.

Play "I Spy." "I spy something that's red and woolly," you might say, describing Chris's favorite sweater. Then let him guess. If he can't get it, give more clues. "It keeps you cozy and warm." Then let him take a turn to describe something he spies for you to guess. (Praise him for being a good describer. We don't want to encourage the child to give wrong descriptions to trick you; we want to encourage good descriptions that help the guesser get the right answer as quickly as possible.)

Language and vocabulary skills are among the most important abilities for getting along well in school and in life. It's not hard to increase your child's abilities in this area. In fact, it's easy—and it's fun!

Intake, Organization, and Memory Skills

In the last few chapters, we have discussed general information, language, and vocabulary skills. All of these are learned skills; your Danny is taking in information that has been generated externally and is increasing his abilities by practice and repetition. Underlying the ability to learn these skills are a number of processes, each of which affects Danny's ability to pick up and absorb and make use of these skills.

1. *Reception*. Is Danny receiving signals from the outside world? Can he see, hear, and physically feel what's going on around him?
2. *Perception*. Having heard, seen, and felt, can Danny's mind accurately record the input? Can he see the differences in colors, shapes, letters, numbers, or hear differences in sounds?
3. *Storage and retrieval*. Having recorded what the senses take in, can Danny remember the information when he needs it? Can he memorize the alphabet? Learn to sing a song?
4. *Attention*. When signals start coming in, is Danny able to watch and listen? Can he pay attention to your voice or the pictures in a story, or is he distracted?

You can see these processes build upon one another. Danny must be able to see and hear and feel in order to register what's going on. What he sees and hears must be perceived accurately and stored properly if he is to remember it correctly. And none of these processes can operate successfully if Danny can't focus attention on the job at hand.

163

To understand how each of these processes can affect learning, picture a child's birthday party. The kids have just finished eating their cake when in bounces Happy the Party Clown. The kids are overjoyed. For the next half hour, Happy tells jokes, sings songs, shows his pet mouse, and gives a puppet show called "Where is Prince Handsome?" Everyone has a wonderful time. But when the children try to tell their parents about the party that night each child's story is different—because at our hypothetical party, each child has a different problem with information processing.

Because Dolores is blind, she doesn't know that Happy has red hair and a purple nose, or that Happy's clown suit was covered with huge polka dots. Colors and shapes don't come into her description at all.

Because Marshall is hard of hearing, he didn't hear Happy whisper, "Let's be very quiet so Spanky the Mouse will come out." Marshall said something loud and frightened Spanky back into Happy's pocket.

Sammy is nearsighted, but his parents haven't found it out yet, so he doesn't wear glasses. He couldn't tell which puppet was handsome and which was ugly because he couldn't see their faces. So the puppet show didn't make too much sense to him.

Dolores, Marshall, and Sammy have difficulties with the reception of information, which makes it difficult for them to learn certain types of materials.

Charlotte is tone deaf, so she can't sing "Twinkle, Twinkle" for her parents, in spite of the fact that Happy spent ten minutes teaching the song. Charlotte has a problem with perception of information. Her mind does not accurately record certain sensory input.

Robbie, on the other hand, saw, heard, and recorded everything, but he just can't quite remember it all. He's not sure whether Happy came in the front door or the back; he can remember the first joke, but he missed the punchline of the second, and he forgot the third one altogether. Robbie has a problem with storage and retrieval of information.

Valerie was able to see and hear what went on, and she'd probably have been able to record and remember it, if only she'd been paying attention. But when Happy told the first joke, Val had an itch on her ankle that took up all her attention; during the second joke, she was too busy trying to unbutton her sweater; on the third joke, she had another itch in the middle of her back that she was trying to get at. Valerie is too easily distracted. She just can't seem to pay attention. In fact, it's all she can do to sit still—she is hyperactive.

PERCEPTION AND MEMORY

Memory can be thought of as a process like preparing food from the garden for freezing. Picking the vegetables from the garden would be like having an experience—listening to a teacher or watching the juggling clown at the circus.

Cutting the veggies is like the process of perception. We cannot actually take in an experience whole: the senses break it down into manageable pieces.

As soon as the veggies are cut up, they are put in the pot to be blanched—just briefly. This is like the short-term memory—holding a thought or an image for just a few seconds.

Then the blanched vegetables are quickly popped into freezer bags and into the freezer chest. Similarly, information from short-term memory is transferred to long-term memory for storage.

The comparison also works well when thinking about remembering information, or recall: recognition, long-term memory, is like a chest-style freezer. Your frozen broccoli can get buried deep down under other things and can be hard to find when you want to get at it. It's the same with ideas. You've had that experience, when you *know* you know someone's name, but you just can't find it in your memory bank.

CRAZY MIXED-UP NUMBERS

This game can help you to determine the accuracy of your child's auditory memory (memory for groups of unrelated words spoken out loud). This skill will come in handy later when your child has to memorize things, such as the days of the week.

Instructions: Say, "I'm going to name some numbers all in the wrong order. Let's see if you can say them back to me just the way I say them." Write down what she says and then score the response. If your child misses three sets in a row, stop, to prevent frustration. Try again at the next age level. (For general scoring instructions, see pages 45–49.)

	Age		
	3½	4½	5½

1. Three–five

		3½	4½	5½
3½	_____	☐		
4½	_____		☐	
5½	_____			☐

2. Two–eight–one

		3½	4½	5½
3½	_____	☐		
4½	_____		☐	
5½	_____			☐

3. Seven–four–three–five

		3½	4½	5½
3½	_____	☐		
4½	_____		☐	
5½	_____			☐

4. Three–eight–one–six–four

		3½	4½	5½
3½	_____	☐		
4½	_____		☐	
5½	_____			☐

THE MEMORY GAME

This old parlor game is fun for kids and can help you get a fix on your child's visual memory (memory for things he or she has seen). This skill will be useful in school when your child is ready to start reading and spelling.

Instructions: Place three familiar items on the table—for instance, a marble, a penny, and a thimble. Tell your child, "I'm going to ask you to close your eyes. Then I'll take one of these things away. When you open your eyes, look at the things left on the table. Then tell me which one I took."

Play the game several times. Then try it with four items, five items, and six items. Play it several times at each level to give your child a chance to perform well. (For general scoring instructions, see pages 45–49.)

	Age		
	3½	4½	5½
1. Child names missing item in set of three	☐	☐	☐
2. Child names missing item in set of four	☐	☐	☐
3. Child names missing item in set of five	☐	☐	☐
4. Child names missing item in set of six	☐	☐	☐

MAKE A NECKLACE

Sequencing and memory are keys to reading, writing, and spelling. This activity provides an early indication of this sequential and memory skill.

Instructions: For this activity, you'll need a number of differently colored wooden beads and two shoestrings. Knot the end of each string; then string several beads in a pattern on one string. Ask your child to make a necklace of beads using the same pattern. Place your necklace out of view while your child performs the task. (For general scoring instructions, see pages 45–49.) *(Continued on next page)*

	Age		
	3½	4½	5½
1. A pattern of one red, one blue, one red, one blue, repeated	☐	☐	☐
2. A pattern of one red, two blue, one red, two blue, repeated	☐	☐	☐
3. A pattern of one red, two blue, one green, repeated	☐	☐	☐
4. A pattern of two green, one red, three blue, repeated	☐	☐	☐

SAY WHAT I SAY

Instructions: This game will show your child's auditory memory for groups of words that make sense. Tell your child to repeat exactly what you say. Consider a response correct if the words are in the correct sequence. Don't worry about mispronunciation. Count an answer wrong if any words are out of sequence or are omitted. If your child responds correctly, place a C (for "correct") on the line after the words. Enter score below. (For general scoring instructions, see pages 45–49.)

	Age		
	3½	4½	5½
1. Doll.	_____	_____	_____
2. Big ball.	_____	_____	_____
3. Run very fast.	_____	_____	_____
4. Mommy makes supper.	_____	_____	_____
5. My little red wagon.	_____	_____	_____
6. Pour me some orange juice.	_____	_____	_____

	Age		
	3½	4½	5½
7. The kitty likes to play with string.	____	____	____
8. Big airplanes fly high in the sky.	____	____	____
9. Horses and cows live out in the country.	____	____	____
10. Tina and Jason like to swim in the summer.	____	____	____
11. On your birthday, you get presents from friends and relatives.	____	____	____
12. Sunny days are good for playing outside, but rainy days are not.	____	____	____

Scoring	3½	4½	5½
Four or five items correct	☐	☐	☐
Six or seven items correct	☐	☐	☐
Eight or nine items correct	☐	☐	☐
Ten or more items correct	☐	☐	☐

PACKING FOR A TRIP

This is another parlor game that's popular with parents and children. Our version is modified to test auditory memory skill.

Instructions: The object is for your child to remember all the things that have been packed. Say each line, and ask your child to repeat it after you. Give a demonstration of how to play the game before you begin. If she forgets three times in a row, stop. Try again at the next age level. (For general scoring instructions, see pages 45–49.)

Say, "I was packing for a trip, and in my suitcase I put . . ."

	Age		
	3½	4½	5½
1. A ball	☐	☐	☐
2. A ball, a flower	☐	☐	☐
3. A ball, a flower, a pin	☐	☐	☐
4. A ball, a flower, a pin, a goat	☐	☐	☐
5. A ball, a flower, a pin, a goat, a bell	☐	☐	☐
6. A ball, a flower, a pin, a goat, a bell, a key	☐	☐	☐
7. A ball, a flower, a pin, a goat, a bell, a key, a doll	☐	☐	☐
8. A ball, a flower, a pin, a goat, a bell, a key, a doll, a hat	☐	☐	☐
9. A ball, a flower, a pin, a goat, a bell, a key, a doll, a hat, an apple	☐	☐	☐

THE NONSENSE GAME

This auditory memory game resembles "Packing for a Trip," but it uses syllables instead of words.

Instructions: Say, "I'm going to say some nonsense words. They don't mean anything at all, but let's see how many you can say back, just the way I say them." Demonstrate once with made-up syllables of your own if your child doesn't understand the instructions. Score a correct answer only if he or she remembers all the syllables in the correct order. (For general scoring instructions, see pages 45–49.)

	Age		
	3½	4½	5½
1. Tat	☐	☐	☐
2. Tat-nip	☐	☐	☐
3. Tat-nip-sim	☐	☐	☐
4. Tat-nip-sim-gof	☐	☐	☐
5. Tat-nip-sim-gof-lex	☐	☐	☐
6. Tat-nip-sim-gof-lex-jub	☐	☐	☐
7. Tat-nip-sim-gof-lex-jub-mim	☐	☐	☐
8. Tat-nip-sim-gof-lex-jub-mim-paz	☐	☐	☐

PICTURE SURPRISES

This visual perception game will show you how well your child deals with figure-ground problems (the ability to select details from a complicated setting). Paying attention to the most important material in a workbook page or in a comic book is important to getting the main idea and making sense of what's presented. It is also important in reading to see the black letters as figures against the white background, not the other way around. For small children, this is not as automatic as it seems.

Instructions: Show your child the picture, and the separate drawings of the items hidden in the picture on page 172. Say, "All of these shapes are hidden in this picture somewhere. Here's one right here. [Show him or her one of the items hidden in the drawing.] Can you find some more? Show me." Most children enjoy the fun of locating the hidden objects. (For scoring instructions, see pages 45–49.)

	Age		
	3½	4½	5½
1. Child finds one to three items	☐	☐	☐
2. Child finds four or five items	☐	☐	☐
3. Child finds six or seven items	☐	☐	☐
4. Child finds eight or nine items	☐	☐	☐

WHAT TO DO WITH YOUR RESULTS

After you've played all the games and done all the tests in this section, take a look at your child's results. If there are a lot of pluses, you know Danny is doing well in these "intake skills," which are such an important base for success in school.

One or two empty boxes are no cause for concern; most children will make occasional mistakes in any game or test. However, if there are a lot of empty boxes, Danny did not do as well as most children would do in these games. You may want to take a closer look at his abilities in the area of "intake" skills.

And if Danny's scoreboard shows a lot of checks and few pluses or empty boxes, his intake abilities lie within the normal range.

If you think there may be some reason for concern, your first stop is the nursery school. Frequently, when a preschooler is having problems, this is the area in which those problems show themselves. After all, looking back over the areas we've already discussed in this book, as a preschooler Danny isn't really expected to *know* very much yet. His language skills aren't supposed to be well developed yet—but he should have the basic abilities necessary to gather information and to learn about language and other areas. And this area—the development of the underlying skills needed for learning—is what the nursery-school teacher is paying the most attention to. If the teacher finds that Danny is inattentive, has a hard time following directions, or always seems to get things out of sequence, he or she will be concerned and will pass that concern on to you.

After your general "How is Danny doing?" opening remark, you might say, "It seems to me that whenever Danny brings home an art project, he has things done in the wrong order. The snowman he did last week had its eyes pasted on *underneath* the head. Is this something I should be concerned about?" A good teacher will know whether Danny's problem shows signs of being a long-term situation, or whether it's just that there is a new assistant this month who hasn't made the explanations clear enough and most of the children in the class have had problems with those art projects.

It often happens that a child who gives every indication of being very bright, but whose performance is considered "erratic," will, in the future, turn out to have a learning disability—a problem with these intake skills of memory or cognition, auditory or visual perception, or attention span. That is why nursery-school teachers pay particular attention to intake skills. If the problem can be detected at an early age, the child and the parents can often avoid a good deal of frustration and misunderstanding.

So if Danny's nursery-school teacher says, "Yes, Danny does seem to have trouble following directions, and he has a short attention span," what's your next step?

A trip to the pediatrician. The first thing to do is to check Danny out physically. Does he see clearly? Hear clearly? The pediatrician can do a quick screening in the office and, if he or she thinks there may be a physical problem, will recommend an ophthalmologist to check Danny's vision in greater detail, or an audiologist to check Danny's hearing.

If the physical exam shows that Danny's eyes and ears are working fine, a sensible next step would be to call your public school or, if your pediatrician recommends it, a child study team to have a preschool screening done on Danny. This screening can help determine the extent to which he is having trouble listening, remembering, following directions, paying attention, and perceiving things with his eyes and ears.

Your public school may have a special-education specialist who will be involved in the evaluation of Danny's visual, spatial, and perceptual abilities. This specialist will be watching to see if Danny has a tendency to perceive things correctly but then mix them up when he tries to explain what he has seen. This is an indication of learning disability—an information-processing problem. At this age, Danny is too young to have his problem *diagnosed*, for instance, as dyslexia—difficulty in reading—or dysgraphia—difficulty in writing. He's too young to read or write! But a tendency to "mixed-upness" may reveal itself. To give a somewhat oversimplified example, if you ask Danny what a dog sounds like and the answer is "It's black and white," you know Danny has confused the words *sound* and *look*. He knows that *sound* doesn't mean *look*, but there's been a glitch in there somewhere. (Incidentally, this can happen to anyone once in a while, and the occasional mix-up shouldn't worry you. It's when this type of mix-up *usually* happens that a long-term problem may be involved.)

What if the physical examination of Danny's eyes and ears reveals that there may be a neurological problem—a dysfunction in Danny's nervous system that interferes with his sight or hearing or other sensory functions? Then you would probably be sent to a pediatric neurologist. He or she would check for actual structural or medically determinable malfunctioning, examining the skull and the spinal column and even the skin. (Because the brain and the skin develop at the same time in the embryo, neurologists have learned that some brain problems can be diagnosed by the presence of certain skin conditions. Brownish "café au lait" spots, for instance, can be a symptom of cerebral palsy.) Neurologists are trained to observe external signs that suggest various conditions. In addition, they can use a variety of sophisticated means to describe and diagnose problems.

WHAT CAN YOU DO?

If you're interested in improving Danny's memory, attention span, and intake skills, there are lots of games you can play that will provide practice in these areas. You can play some of the games from the test section of this chapter, for instance. Many of them are great car games for long trips.

To help Danny practice auditory perception, try the following activity.

Gather a variety of materials, such as rice, sand, macaroni, pebbles, and flour. Put several spoonfuls of each in a bag. Make duplicate sets of bags—two with flour, two with rice, and so on. Make sure the bags are not transparent, so there will be no visual clue. Have him shake a bag from set A; then ask him to find the bag in set B that sounds the same. (Older children may have fun trying to name what's in each bag. Younger children—under four and a half—will probably find naming the materials beyond them, but they should have a good time finding the sounds that match.) If you haven't got enough small bags, cans or plastic margarine tubs will work.

Play "Match My Music." Sing a note, and have your child sing the same note. After a while, try two notes, then three. You may even be able to work up to a simple, made-up tune. If you like, you can help Danny put words to the tune, just for the fun of writing your own song.

For practice in visual perception, you can start with some simple household jobs. Let Danny help you with the laundry by sorting the socks according to color and/or size. Ask him to put away the silverware when you put the clean dishes away. Get out the silverware tray and put one knife, one fork, and one spoon in the correct place. Then let him finish the job. Not only is this good training for visual perception, it also gives him a feeling of being needed—and a little help with the dishes can't hurt!

When you and Danny are cleaning up his room, ask him to sort out the books and put the little ones on the top shelf and the big ones on the bottom. Then sort each shelf by color—blue books first, then red, then green. You can even sort the clothes in the closet by colors.

Here's another matching game that has its own built-in reward: You and your child can make cookies using cookie cutters in different shapes. When Danny correctly matches two similarly shaped cookies, let him eat the fruits of his labor!

You can probably come up with other games to help sharpen your child's visual and auditory acuity and strengthen his memory. And you'll find that these games are as much fun for you as they are for your child.

□9□

Motor Skills Measurement

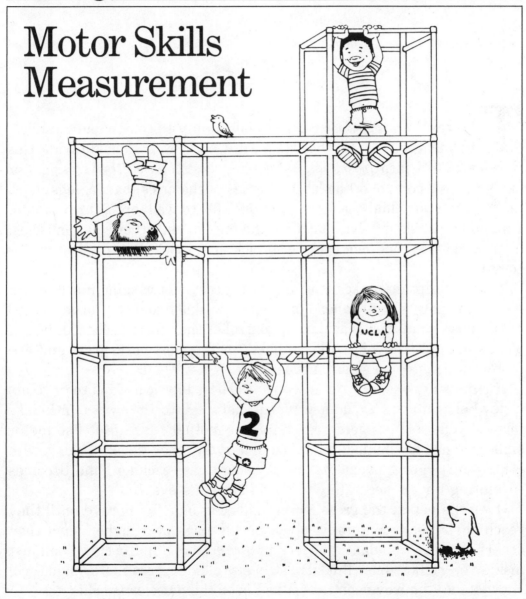

The term *motor skills* refers to our ability to control our muscles, to make our bodies do what we want. Professionals divide this physical ability into *gross motor skills* and *fine motor skills*. Gross motor skills involve control of the large muscles of the arms, hands, legs, feet, and body. Your child uses gross motor skills to walk or to throw a ball. Fine motor skills involve control of the fingers and other small muscles. Your child uses fine motor skills to pick up a block—or to stick out his tongue!

This description makes it sound as if gross motor skills must be developed separately and ahead of fine motor skills, and that once control of the larger muscles is achieved, control of the fine muscles can begin. That's not quite how it works. In fact, for the most part, gross and fine motor skills develop simultaneously.

A child's gross motor skills are the earliest physical skills to develop: a newborn infant's random wavings mature into the two-month-old's intent-eyed, splay-fingered reach for her mother's face. But fine motor skills are not far behind, and once underway, they develop along with control of larger movements. Pretty soon that reaching hand becomes a pointing finger, accurately poked in Mother's eye.

Over the years, the gross motor skills continue to improve until they reach their peak. Naturally, some people peak at a higher level than others. We can't all dance the lead in *Swan Lake* or put a curve ball just inside the strike zone. But almost every child's gross motor skills will show steady improvement as control over the muscles is achieved.

Some people will be better at gross motor skills than fine, and vice versa. There are football heroes who can't thread a needle, and prize-winning embroiderers who can't cross a room without stumbling over their needlework baskets. And of course there are those fortunate, well-coordinated ones who excel at both gross and fine motor skills. Roosevelt Grier is one football hero who is also famous for his needlepoint. It's all a matter of individual difference.

The development of motor skills follows a specific sequence, although the timing varies from one individual to another. It will proceed from the head down to the feet and from the trunk of the body out to the fingers and toes. Thus, John can lift his head before he can knock a toy out of his playpen, and he can wave bye-bye with his whole arm before he can wave his fingers.

GROSS MOTOR SKILLS

Gross motor skills usually follow a predictable pattern of development. Take the twins Melanie and Martin, for instance. Their mother has kept careful records of their physical progress, and she has been intrigued by the fact that, although sometimes Melanie progressed faster than Martin, and sometimes Martin surged ahead of Melanie, they mastered the skills in the same sequence.

Both children could, at the age of three, walk along a ten-foot chalk line on the sidewalk with a minimum of mistakes. (Martin stepped off twice; Melanie, once.) They could also walk upstairs, one foot to a step—as long as there was a railing to hold on to. But for coming down, it was two feet to a step, and hold that railing tight! (Why it should be easier to go up than to come down was a mystery to Mother until she tried it herself with a large load of laundry. It's easier to balance when you can lean forward—and you can't lean forward when you're going down-stairs!)

During their third year, both children mastered the arts of standing on tiptoe and standing on one foot—however briefly. (Melanie, always better at balancing activities than Martin, could hold the pose longer than her brother.) Both of them could jump and land with their feet together—a skill particularly well-suited to squashing beetles.

Probably because his father took an active interest in teaching Martin to play ball, Martin learned to kick a soccer ball and throw a basketball earlier than Melanie, but they both had mastered these skills well before the end of their third year. Neither of them, however, could bounce a ball—or catch a bounced ball—until they were four, and even then it was not so much a matter of catching the ball as of trapping it between hands and chest. Still, their father wasn't about to complain. It was a step in the right direction!

For their fourth birthdays, Melanie and Martin each got a tricycle, and they began to take pleasure in climbing on the jungle gym at school.

Now they could stand on one foot for a full five seconds, run without falling, walk up the stairs without hanging on to the railing, and—at last!—go downstairs one foot to a step. They still needed to hold on to the railing, though. Not until they were five did they feel secure enough to walk down the stairs without holding on to something.

Five was the year when they learned to skip—sort of. Unable to skip on alternate feet, they ended up doing a skip-step, skip-step kind of thing, like a sailor with a wooden leg. They were both pretty good at hopping, too. Melanie could hop along for about the length of the sofa, and Martin could go almost as far. Martin quickly learned to throw the basketball, using both hands, and to catch it with both hands when his dad bounced it back to him. Melanie was only a few months older than Martin when she mastered that skill.

By the time they were six, they had enough control over their bodies to skip properly, to stand on one foot for ten seconds, to catch a tennis ball when their dad bounced it to them, and to take part in various playground games, from jumprope to roller skating.

Although Melanie and Martin did not master these gross motor skills at exactly the same time, they were within a few months of each other—and the majority of children between three and five master the same skills in the same order. It's a matter of gaining control over the arms, legs, hands, and feet.

FINE MOTOR SKILLS

Like gross motor skills, fine motor skills usually follow a certain pattern of development. When Melanie and Martin were three, they had enough control over their fingers to string large wooden beads on a heavy string. It took several minutes to string three or four beads, but with concentration they could do it. They could hold a crayon and copy a circle—not too accurately, but close enough. They had learned how to use scissors but could only snip with them; they couldn't cut out a figure. (Melanie was quicker to control scissors than Martin.)

By the time she was four, Melanie could copy a straight line and a cross, and she could draw a person with two parts—a head and legs. (Her father thought it was Humpty Dumpty.) What's more, she could build a tower of nine blocks, and to her mother's relief, she was able to wind up her own music box. She could also use her scissors to cut up a piece of paper—or a magazine. Martin kept right up with his sister.

When they were four, they could put together a jigsaw puzzle their grandmother had given them—one that came in a wooden tray and had six pieces. Melanie developed this skill slightly ahead of Martin, but only by a few weeks.

At five, their puzzles could have as many as eight pieces, and their towers held up to ten blocks. They could copy a square and a triangle, and draw a person with seven parts—a person that anyone could recognize as human. They could even draw a house right next to the person, but the house was likely to be (like the Grinch's heart) "two sizes too small." Proportion means nothing to a five-year-old child. What really matters at that age is making sure Daddy's picture has really long legs.

Melanie was five when she learned to copy some simple capital letters such as V, H, and O, and Martin was right on her trail. It was another year before they graduated to lowercase letters. At six, too, they could print their names—slowly, carefully, and unevenly, running very much downhill. They could copy the numbers from one to ten, and if they made a mistake, they could erase them and do it over again. They could also sharpen their own pencils.

Your child may achieve some or all of these skills sooner or later than Melanie and Martin, but it is most likely that the progression will be the same, as your child builds one skill upon another to grow and learn.

WHY IS MEASURING MOTOR SKILLS IMPORTANT?

Your child's brain and nervous system are growing and developing rapidly. In the preschool years, intellectual and physical development are closely linked. Motor development in young children reflects not only their physical pattern of growth and development but also, indirectly, their cognitive development. The nervous system controls not only our muscles but our thinking, too. Early muscle coordination indicates to some degree the way in which other nervous functions are developing. This is a tenuous connection—not 100 percent reliable—but it's one of the few indicators that are available for preschool children, since we can't open them up and check out their nervous systems under a microscope. That's why gross motor or large-muscle control and fine motor or small-muscle control can be good indicators of the child's growth and development. Moreover, motor activities are one of the best ways of learning about the world, gathering information, and solving problems. When Alison builds a tower of blocks, she's exhibiting more than the physical dexterity required to balance those little squares of wood; she's also showing that she understands how to get a taller tower. She's "thinking with her hands."

To watch and record your child's development in the area of motor skills, try the games, activities, and observations we've suggested below.

GROSS MOTOR ACTIVITIES

Most skills included in the gross motor section can be observed in your house, in your backyard, or at the playground, without the need to set up special situations.

FOLLOW THE LEADER

Instructions: First read over the list of abilities included in this game to familiarize yourself with the skills to be checked. Then say to your child, "Let's play Follow the Leader. You be the leader, and take me into every room of the house." (Your goal is to get the child to lead you up the stairs and down again. If there are no stairs in your home, play the game in a place where there are stairs.)

Play the game for several minutes. You may even want to play it more than once on different days to make sure you have a good feel for your child's skill at walking, running, and climbing stairs. When you have finished playing the game, score your child's performance in the boxes. (For general scoring instructions, see pages 45–49.)

	Age		
	3½	4½	5½
1. The child walks upstairs, alternating feet, with rail support.	☐	☐	☐
2. The child walks downstairs with rail support, two feet to a step.	☐	☐	☐
3. The child walks upstairs, alternating feet, without rail support.	☐	☐	☐
4. The child walks downstairs, alternating feet, with rail support.	☐	☐	☐
5. The child walks downstairs, alternating feet, without rail support.	☐	☐	☐

FOLLOW THE LEADER AGAIN

Instructions: This time it's your turn to be the leader. Read over the list of skills in the section and be sure to include each one as you lead your child through the activities. For example, you might start by skipping around the table, hopping into the living room, doing a broad jump, and standing on one foot for five to ten seconds. Then you could do another sequence including some more skills. Note that one activity involves walking along a straight line for ten feet. If you are playing indoors, you might be able to use a floor board or the edge of a row of tiles for your line. If not, you may be able to set out a ten-foot stretch of masking tape. This won't harm your carpet if it is picked up soon after you finish the game. Of course, if you're playing outdoors, you can chalk a line on the sidewalk. Or use your imagination to come up with your own ten-foot line. Remember to lead your child through each activity, even those that she is not expected to perform at her age. (For general scoring instructions, see pages 45–49.)

	Age		
	3½	4½	5½
1. Child skips on one foot	☐	☐	☐
2. Child skips on alternate feet	☐	☐	☐
3. Child stands on one foot momentarily	☐	☐	☐
4. Child stands on tiptoe momentarily	☐	☐	☐
5. Child jumps and lands with both feet together	☐	☐	☐
6. Child broad jumps twelve inches, landing with feet together	☐	☐	☐
7. Child stands on one foot for five seconds	☐	☐	☐
8. Child stands on one foot for ten seconds	☐	☐	☐
9. Child walks backward heel-to-toe	☐	☐	☐
10. Child hops forward on one foot for six feet	☐	☐	☐
11. Child walks on a clearly marked line for ten feet, placing one foot in front of the other, stepping off the line no more than two times	☐	☐	☐

PLAY BALL!

Instructions: This one is easy. You'll need two balls—a playground ball about twelve inches in diameter and a tennis ball. All you have to do is take your child outside on a nice day, or clear a space inside the house if it's winter, and play with the balls. Be sure you read over the list of items in this section so you'll know what to watch for as you play. If your child has trouble catching, use balls made of spongy material, such as a Nerf ball. (For general scoring instructions, see pages 45–49.)

	Age		
	3½	4½	5½
1. Child kicks a large ball forward while standing in place	☐	☐	☐
2. Child throws a large ball forward using underhand motions	☐	☐	☐
3. Child catches a bounced playground ball with hands and chest	☐	☐	☐
4. Child bounces a large ball two times with both hands	☐	☐	☐
5. Child throws a large ball from chest with both hands	☐	☐	☐
6. Child catches a bounced playground ball with both hands	☐	☐	☐
7. Child catches a bounced tennis ball with both hands	☐	☐	☐

PLAYGROUND ACTIVITIES

Instructions: After reading through the list of items in this section, take your child to a park or playground, or observe him at nursery school playing on the equipment there. He will probably need no encouragement to do the activities listed because these are the things children do at the playground. But if your child shows hesitation, you can suggest an activity and offer to stand by to help "just in case you want me to." Don't urge your child to do something he is unsure that he can do—simply leave the box for that item blank. (For general scoring instructions, see pages 45–49.)

	Age		
	3½	4½	5½
1. Child climbs playground jungle gym	☐	☐	☐
2. Child rides tricycle	☐	☐	☐
3. Child rides small bike with training wheels	☐	☐	☐
4. Child climbs overhead playground ladder	☐	☐	☐
5. Child rides small bike without training wheels	☐	☐	☐

GENERAL GROSS MOTOR SKILLS

Instructions: These are activities that most children take an interest in, so all you need to do is provide a jumprope, skates, and some music. If your child has never tried one of these activities, you can offer instructions and demonstrations, but don't urge her beyond her capabilities. (For general scoring instructions, see pages 45–49.)

	Age		
	3½	4½	5½
1. Child jumps rope for four consecutive jumps	☐	☐	☐
2. Child begins to roller skate	☐	☐	☐
3. Child dances to music	☐	☐	☐

FINE MOTOR SKILLS

CLAY SHAPES

Instructions: Give your child a nice lump of modeling clay that he or she can comfortably squeeze. (Don't use soft Play-Doh. Use regular modeling clay. You'll have to knead the clay to soften it a bit first.) Watch your child knead and manipulate the clay. Then ask him or her to make the shapes listed below. If your youngster doesn't understand some or all of the shapes, you can demonstrate once. (For general scoring instructions, see pages 45–49.)

	Age		
	3½	4½	5½
1. Child makes a ball	☐	☐	☐
2. Child makes a "snake"	☐	☐	☐
3. Child makes a "pancake"	☐	☐	☐
4. Child makes a snowman	☐	☐	☐
5. Child makes a basket with handle	☐	☐	☐
6. Child makes a dog (standing on four legs)	☐	☐	☐

STRING AND BEADS

Instructions: For these games you will need two eighteen-inch shoestrings and half a dozen small (half-inch) wooden beads. Ask your child to watch you tie a simple knot in the lace. Then hand the other lace to your child and ask her to tie a knot like the one you tied.

	Age		
	3½	4½	5½
1. Child ties a single knot in a shoelace	☐	☐	☐

(Continued on next page)

Now ask your child to string the beads on the shoelace. (Note: there should be one knot in the lace, at the end, to keep the beads from slipping off.) If your child can string six beads in less than two minutes, place a check in the box. For general scoring instructions, see pages 45–49.)

	Age		
	3½	4½	5½
2. Child successfully strings six beads	☐	☐	☐

SNIP A PICTURE

Instructions: For this activity, you'll need colorful construction paper, a pair of primary scissors, and glue. Look over the skills to be observed so you'll know what you are testing for. Then tell your child that you're going to make pictures out of shapes. Draw some circles and squares, and make a few lines all the way across the paper about an inch apart. Ask your child to cut along the lines so you will have some circles, squares, and strips of paper to make your pictures. When the shapes have been cut out, you and your child may use them in any way you like to create pictures. (For general scoring instructions, see pages 45–49.)

	Age		
	3½	4½	5½
1. Child makes snips in the edge of the paper	☐	☐	☐
2. Child cuts continuously along a line	☐	☐	☐
3. Child cuts on a curve	☐	☐	☐
4. Child pastes shapes on paper where you indicate	☐	☐	☐

WINDMILL

Instructions: For this activity, you'll need two square pieces of paper, a pair of primary scissors, a pencil with a good eraser on the end, and a pin.

First read over the list of skills at the end of this activity so that you'll know what abilities you're looking for. Then tell your child that you're going to make a windmill.

Begin by folding one piece of paper diagonally to make a triangle (1). Ask your child to do the same with his identical piece of paper. Then fold the paper again to make a smaller triangle (2), and ask your child to do the same.

Now unfold the paper. Tell your child to cut along the fold lines almost to the middle of the paper (3). (If he does not understand, you may demonstrate once.)

With the pin, pierce every other point to the center (4). Then push the pin into the eraser of the pencil (5). Ask your child to do the same. When this is done, you've made a windmill. Ask your child to blow on it, and see what happens (6).

Younger children may experience more difficulty with this activity than older ones. Let your child attempt each of the steps. If at any point your child is unable to complete one of the steps, you can complete that step for him. (For general scoring instructions, see pages 45–49.)

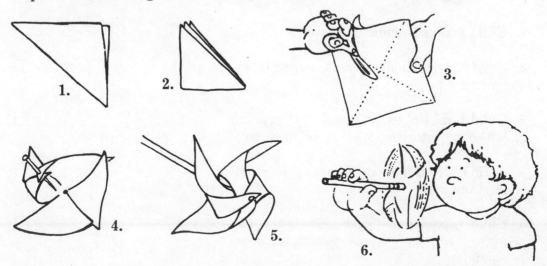

(Continued on next page)

	Age		
	3½	4½	5½
1. Child folds paper diagonally	☐	☐	☐
2. Child makes second diagonal fold	☐	☐	☐
3. Child unfolds paper	☐	☐	☐
4. Child cuts along fold lines almost to middle of paper	☐	☐	☐
5. Child pierces every other point to center	☐	☐	☐

PLAYING "FONZIE"

Instructions: Ask your child to make a thumbs-up gesture like The Fonz does (a fist with the thumb sticking up). Say, "Fonzie says, 'Wiggle your thumb!' " Then demonstrate the other skills and ask the child to do them one at a time. (For general scoring instructions, see pages 45–49.)

	Age		
	3½	4½	5½
1. Child makes thumbs-up gesture	☐	☐	☐
2. Child wiggles thumb without moving other fingers	☐	☐	☐
3. Child blinks eyes open and shut rapidly without contorting other facial muscles	☐	☐	☐
4. Child sticks tongue in and out rapidly and rhythmically	☐	☐	☐
5. Child taps index finger and thumb together rapidly without moving arm or shoulder	☐	☐	☐

BUILDING A TOWER

Instructions: For this activity, you'll need twelve square alphabet blocks. Place a block in front of your child. Start stacking them one on top of another until the stack is three blocks high. Then say, "You finish the tower. See how high you can go." (For general scoring instructions, see pages 45–49.)

	Age		
	3½	4½	5½
1. Child stacks five blocks	☐	☐	☐
2. Child stacks eight blocks	☐	☐	☐
3. Child stacks twelve blocks	☐	☐	☐

JIGSAW PUZZLE

Instructions: Get some simple jigsaw puzzles made of wood or heavy cardboard, the kind that fit into their own tray-frame. You'll need three puzzles: one with four to five pieces, one with six to eight pieces, and one with more than eight pieces. Offer them to your child; if necessary, show her how puzzles are put together. Then let the child complete the puzzle herself. Note: The puzzles should not be familiar to the child. (For general scoring instructions, see pages 45–49.)

	Age		
	3½	4½	5½
1. Child completes a four-to-five-piece puzzle	☐	☐	☐
2. Child completes a six-to-eight-piece puzzle	☐	☐	☐
3. Child completes a more-than-eight-piece puzzle	☐	☐	☐

WIND-UPS

Instructions: This is an easy one. Hand your child a wind-up toy or music box, and ask him to wind it as far as he can. Then let the wind-up toy do its thing! (For general scoring instructions, see pages 45–49.)

	Age		
	3½	4½	5½
Child winds toy completely without stopping. (This may take several twists.)	☐	☐	☐

PAPER AND PENCIL GAMES

Instructions: For these activities, you'll need a pencil with an eraser on the end and some paper. Read through the list of skills so you'll be familiar with them. Then hand the pencil and paper to your child. Ask her to sharpen the pencil and write some letters—any letters she wants. Or you may want to ask her to write her name (whether you think this is a familiar task or not). (For general scoring instructions, see pages 45–49.)

	Age		
	3½	4½	5½
1. Child can successfully use a manual pencil sharpener	☐	☐	☐
2. Child makes lines or shapes of any kind	☐	☐	☐
3. Child makes any recognizable letter	☐	☐	☐
4. Child makes four or five well-formed letters	☐	☐	☐
5. Child can successfully use a pencil eraser	☐	☐	☐

COPYCATS

Instructions: Pictured below is a group of shapes. Have your child copy the shapes. Give your child some paper and a pencil and ask her to copy each shape. (For general scoring instructions, see pages 45–49.)

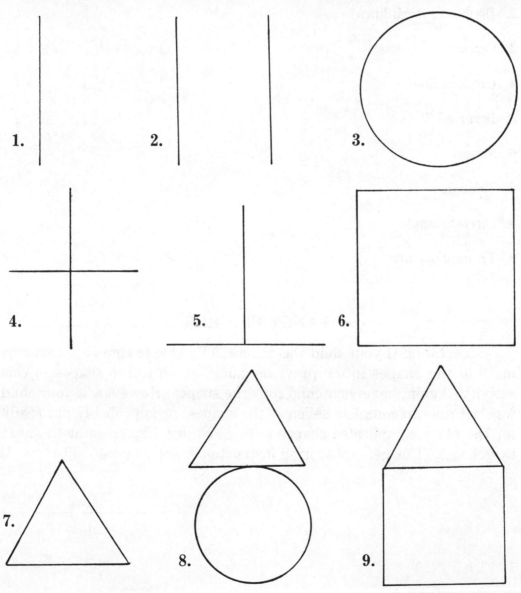

1.

2.

3.

4.

5.

6.

7.

8.

9.

(Continued on next page)

	Age		
	3½	4½	5½
1. Vertical line	☐	☐	☐
2. Double vertical lines	☐	☐	☐
3. Circle	☐	☐	☐
4. Crossed lines	☐	☐	☐
5. Inverted T	☐	☐	☐
6. Square	☐	☐	☐
7. Triangle	☐	☐	☐
8. Circle/triangle	☐	☐	☐
9. Triangle/square	☐	☐	☐

FANCY FIGURES

Instructions: If your child was successfully able to complete seven or more of the shapes in the previous game, go on to the shapes in this activity. Again, have your child copy the shapes. However, if your child was not able to complete seven of the shapes, he is probably not ready for the more complicated shapes in this activity. Try them at the next target age. (For general scoring instructions, see pages 45–49.)

	Age		
	3½	4½	5½
1. Fish	☐	☐	☐
2. Smile face	☐	☐	☐

	Age		
	3½	4½	5½
3. Double square	☐	☐	☐
4. Diamond in square	☐	☐	☐
5. Sailboat	☐	☐	☐
6. Flower	☐	☐	☐

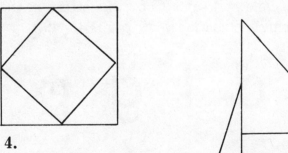

1.

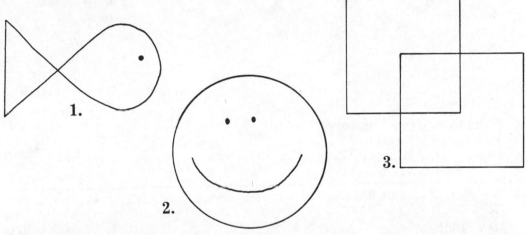

2.

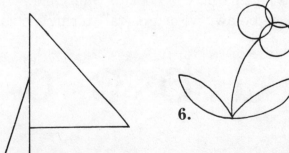

3.

4.

5.

6.

NUMBERS AND LETTERS

Instructions: Look at the numbers from one through ten. Give your child some paper and a pencil and say, "Copy these numbers that you see here." (For general scoring instructions, see pages 45–49.)

$$1 \quad 2 \quad 3 \quad 4 \quad 5$$
$$6 \quad 7 \quad 8 \quad 9 \quad 10$$

	Age		
	3½	4½	5½
1. Child copies two numbers	☐	☐	☐
2. Child copies five or more numbers	☐	☐	☐
3. Child copies eight or more numbers	☐	☐	☐

Now look at the page where the letters, a, b, c, d, f, g, and p are shown. (These are letters made of both curved and straight lines.) Hand the pencil and the book to your child and say, "Copy the letters in the space below." (For general scoring instructions, see pages 45–49.)

$$a \quad b \quad c \quad d \quad f \quad g \quad p$$

	Age		
	3½	4½	5½
1. Child draws two letters	☐	☐	☐
2. Child draws four letters	☐	☐	☐
3. Child draws six letters	☐	☐	☐

WHAT TO DO WITH YOUR RESULTS

Okay, you've finished the motor skills and games. Now you know that your Mike is high, midrange, or low in motor skills. What can you do about it?

If he has checks in most of the boxes, his scoring is in the broad midrange of normal ability. Just keep on doing what you've been doing. Mike is coming along fine. There will be plenty of kids in the neighborhood who are more agile and athletic than he is, but you know he's no slouch either, and he should always be able to compete on an equal basis with his friends.

If he scores a lot of pluses in motor skills, terrific! You'll want to encourage him in any special interests and offer plenty of opportunities for skating or soccer, if that's where his heart lies. But here's a word of warning: Don't expect too much. At this age, it's too early for you to assume that you're raising a future gold-medal winner. Many children who rate high in motor skills at three or four years will eventually reach a plateau, a point at which they level off. Then they wait on that plateau while other kids catch up to them, and they go on to be perfectly normal in their motor skills. If this happens to Mike, be reassured. It's not that he has lost the magic; it's just that he is following a pattern that many children follow, a pattern of early achievement followed by more normal development.

And what if Mike has a lot of empty boxes in the motor skill games? Is there anything you can do?

Indeed there is. In fact, motor skills is an area in which you can almost certainly do something concrete to help.

First, though, let's get some second opinions on Mike's physical abilities. Talk to his nursery-school teachers.

Start with the general, open-ended question: "How is Mike doing in school?" If the teachers say, "He's doing fine, except for some problems with riding the trikes," that's a significant answer. They have volunteered the information that they have the same concerns you do and have noticed some clearly observable problems.

However, if the teachers respond to your opening question with "Oh, fine. He's having a great time!" or some equally general remark, you can zero in with, "It sometimes seems to me that Mike has a problem keeping up with the other kids in running and climbing. Have you noticed that?" This will encourage the teachers to come forth with more detailed observations, without fear of wounding or irritating you.

Now Mike's teachers may say, "No, as a matter of fact, Mike really seems to keep up pretty well motorwise." In which case you may decide to wait and watch and, in a few weeks or months, try the tests again and see if Mike's score has gone up. There's always the chance you caught him on a bad day, or perhaps you were trying the tests too soon. You might also ask the nursery school to keep a special watch to see if they begin to notice any motor difficulties.

But what if Mike's teachers say, "Oh, I'm glad you brought that up, because we have been a little concerned."

In that case, the next thing to do is talk to your pediatrician. Again start with general questions and then, if need be, zero in on your specific concern. Tell the doctor you've noticed that your child seems to be lagging behind the other kids in motor skills, and that the nursery school has observed the same thing. (If your child doesn't go to nursery school, you can begin by consulting the pediatrician.) If the pediatrician has not seen Mike recently, he or she will probably want you to bring him in for a checkup to confirm your impression. If Mike has had a recent checkup, the doctor may be able to tell you immediately whether there is cause for concern.

At that point, the pediatrician may do one of two things. He or she may say, "Let's keep an eye on Mike for a while and see how he develops." You must realize that what the doctor means is that *you* must keep an eye on Mike and, in a few months, bring his case to your doctor's attention again.

Or the pediatrician may feel that further testing is called for. In this case, the doctor may choose to do the testing personally, or he or she may refer you to one of two types of specialists: a child psychologist or a pediatric neurologist.

Child psychologists specialize in child development. There are developmental psychologists—specializing in normal and abnormal growth and development—and clinical psychologists with a strong background in the area of child development (rather than emotional disturbances).

Child psychologists may be connected with the public school system, with a university that has a program in developmental psychology, with a clinic, or they may be in private practice.

Pediatric neurologists are medical doctors specializing in children's nervous systems. They may be associated with a hospital or a clinic, or they may be in private practice.

The first thing a pediatric neurologist will do is perform some simple tests and informal observations in the office to determine if more complex testing is warranted. (The most common follow-up tests for this purpose include electroencephalograms [EEGs], X-rays, and CAT scans.) If the medical specialists identify a specific condition or disease that is affecting Mike's motor skills, they will prescribe a treatment designed to deal with the problem.

If, however, the problem seems to have no definite physical cause but is instead attributable to a lag in development or to a nonspecific condition, your doctor may counsel patience while Mike continues to develop. Time and growth may bring some improvement, or may reveal a specific cause for which treatment can be prescribed. Parental encouragement and support are the most important factors for the child who is developing at a rate slower than others.

You will notice that we have suggested that you consult your pediatrician before resorting to specialists. If you don't have a pediatrician, you could go directly to one of the specialists we have mentioned. However, we strongly recommend that if you don't have a pediatrician, now is the time to find one. It pays to have a medical practitioner who is familiar with you, your child, and your child's rate and style of development.

AND NOW?

If Mike is not as advanced as his peers in motor skills, what can you do?

You can begin by adjusting your expectations of Mike and helping him to lower his own expectations to a reasonable level. Without putting him down, help him to understand that it's okay if he can't walk a balance beam—there are lots of other things he can do.

But there is no need to give up, to assume that "once a fumble-fist, always a fumble-fist." Even a clumsy child will continue to develop increased motor skills, and these skills improve faster with practice.

ENHANCING MOTOR SKILLS

Whether Mike scored high, middle, or low on the motor skills games, here are some activities that can increase physical agility and dexterity. Most of them are games and crafts you'll remember from your own childhood. You enjoyed them—and so will Mike.

GROSS MOTOR ACTIVITIES

Dodge ball. You need a biggish ball for this game, at least six inches in diameter. If only two are playing, a wall is also helpful to bounce the ball back. If three or more are playing, the wall isn't necessary; one of the players can act as catcher. One person throws the ball (not too hard!), trying to hit another player. The object, of course, is not to be hit. If a player is hit, it's his turn to throw the ball and try to catch another player. (If lots of players are available, the game can be played by teams.

One team throws the ball while the other dodges. When all the dodgers have been tagged out, the teams switch places.) Both throwing and dodging the ball can help children develop increased agility. Remember to take it easy with smaller children; don't expect a three-year-old to stop on a dime. You can build a certain amount of success into the game for toddlers by "telegraphing" your moves—giving them every chance to see where you're about to throw the ball so they'll have plenty of time to avoid it.

Beanbags. It's easy to sew up a few beanbags—just stitch four-inch squares of cloth on three sides, turn them inside out to make bags, fill them half full of beans, and finish the stitching. A younger child can play catch with the bags—they are easier to grab than a ball, and they don't have that annoying tendency to run away from you if you miss them. Older children can try tossing the bags at targets—coffee cans or circles chalked on the sidewalk will do the trick.

Stilts. Five-year-olds can try walking on stilts. Don't expect too much success at this age, but let Mike know that with practice he can learn to take a few steps on stilts.

As an alternative to standard stilts, you can make "tin-can stilts." Punch two holes across from each other on the bottom of the sides of matched coffee cans. Run a long heavy cord or light line through the holes in each can, and tie the ends together. The string must be long enough so Mike can grab it when he stands on the cans with arms down at his sides. To walk, the child stands on the cans and pulls up with the string at each step. This requires coordination of arms and legs and is good practice for gross motor ability.

In general, give Mike every opportunity to ride trikes, bikes, scooters, and the like. Get a wagon so he can take turns getting and giving rides. Take every chance you can to go to the playground; encourage your child to swing on the swings, slide on the slides, and play Tarzan on the jungle gym. The best way to *increase* gross motor skills is to *use* gross motor skills. This means lots of active physical play. If your youngster doen't really enjoy this type of activity, try to at least involve him in fifteen to twenty minutes' worth every day. Play the games yourself to encourage Mike's participation. But remember that it's supposed to be fun, not work. Don't force Mike to do something he truly doesn't enjoy. Look for other activities instead.

FINE MOTOR ACTIVITIES

Painting. Painting is a fun way to increase fine motor activities. Just supply Mike with paints and brushes (with an underlay of newspapers to protect your house!); and let him go to town. If he likes painting in coloring books, fine. If not, give him blank paper and let his imagination take over.

If the paintbrush is difficult to manipulate, try giving him a puddle of poster paint and a piece of sponge to dip into it and spread paint with. If your heart fails you at the thought of liquid poster paint, try a mound of dry poster paint and a damp sponge.

Fingerpaints are a marvelously messy way to really get into your subject. They can be expensive, though, so here's a recipe for homemade fingerpaints. You need a puddle of liquid laundry starch, a spoonful of powdered poster paint, and glossy white shelf paper. Mix the paint and the starch right on the paper, or let your child do the mixing and continue right on into the painting. Fingerpaints encourage gross motor skills (sweeping the whole arm across the page to make a smooth swath of color) as well as fine motor skills (using one finger to make circles and squiggly lines).

By the way, washing the hands and arms can be another way to develop motor skills!

Sewing cards. Sewing cards (pictures with holes punched around the drawings to outline with shoelace "thread") can be purchased at any toy store. You can make your own by pasting pictures to cardboard and punching holes around the object with a paper punch. A shoelace makes an excellent needle and thread, as long as the hard tip is still functioning. Guiding the thread in and out of the holes is great practice for fine motor skills. Stringing beads, just as you did for the games in this section of the book, is also fun. Empty spools make good substitute beads, particularly after you've had the fun of painting them all different colors. Uncooked pasta can also be painted and strung, and it has the added attraction of all those different shapes and sizes, from macaroni to manicotti and rigatoni.

Clay. Modeling shapes with clay is a terrific fine motor activity. Just squishing a soft lump of clay into the hand is extremely satisfying, even if your young sculptor never gets around to making a recognizable shape.

Clay and Play-Doh can be purchased at toy stores, but here's a recipe for modeling dough that can be baked and kept for posterity. Add four cups of flour and one cup of salt to about one and a half cups of water (enough to make a firm, nonsticky dough); just mix the ingredients together (or better yet, let your youngster do the mixing). Small, flattish creations can be baked on a cookie sheet for about half an hour at 350 degrees. If the objets d'art are more than three inches thick, bake at 325 degrees for an hour. The baked pieces can be painted with regular watercolors.

If you prefer the kind of modeling clay that is not baked, add about one-fourth cup of salad oil to the recipe above. Store unused dough in a plastic bag in the refrigerator; it should stay pliable for several weeks.

Stone faces. This activity combines gross and fine motor skills. Collect several round, smooth stones that might make good faces. First have Mike put on rubber gloves and paint the stones white, pink, yellow, or brown, or any good face color. Use water-based paint for easy cleanup and a two-inch brush.

When this layer of paint has dried, older children can paint eyes, ears, noses, and mouths on the stones. The faces can be made to look happy, sad, or any way you please. (Don't expect recognizable faces from three-year-olds or most four-year-olds. The kids might recognize their efforts as human, but you won't.)

In general, just look around the house. Some of the best motor-skill activities take place in the kitchen. When you're making a cake, let your child measure, sift, and stir. Kids love to cook. Take advantage!

A word of warning, though. Kids don't have very long attention spans. It doesn't work well to say "Hey, let's make cookies!"and then go get the flour, the baking pans, and everything else. By the time you have all the ingredients assembled, your budding cook will probably be next door playing with the neighbor's kid. Instead, first set up the equipment and get out the ingredients, then say, "Hey, Mike, want to make some cookies?" Mike will be ready to get to work that very instant, and so will you.

Kids are great at mixing meat loaf with their hands, stirring mashed potatoes, and mixing scrambled eggs. It doesn't have to be cookies or candy or cake—they love anything that has to do with food. (Even if they don't like eating meat loaf, they usually enjoy mushing it around in the bowl!)

The activities we've suggested are just some of the ways you can put Mike's gross and fine motor skills to work and to play. You'll think of more yourself. Just remember this important rule of thumb: Offer Mike plenty of opportunities to get physical on his own level. Don't put him in a gymnastics class with kids whose development is more advanced; this won't help his coordination, and it may only make him more painfully aware of his own clumsiness. A child can't practice skills that he is not ready for. But when he begins to show some slight degree of control over the baseball, that is the time to get out there in the yard and encourage him to play catch as much as he will. Those skills will improve faster with this kind of practice and encouragement, and Mike's gains will be solid, comfortable gains. And that's your goal—to maximize your child's potential.

◻ **10** ◻

Gauging
Personality

The concept of personality is about as easy to get a grip on as a soaped-up baby. Personality is an elusive and changing combination of behaviors and feelings that are repeatedly expressed in similar ways so that they become associated with a particular individual. All these feelings and behaviors become a personality when they form a fairly consistent pattern by which an individual can be recognized.

Naturally, the very core of the concept of personality is that each person has his or her own, and that every individual's personality differs from everyone else's. Johnny Carson's is different from Barbara Walters's; Mick Jagger's is different from Dolly Parton's; Donald Duck's is different from Porky Pig's.

So if you can't get a good grip on the concept, and if personality is different in each of us, how can you measure it?

You can't.

You can only measure some indicators and make guesses based on those measurements. Educated guesses, based on psychologists' many years of observing different personalities, but only guesses nonetheless.

Okay, once you've made your educated guesses, what can you do about personality? Can you change it? Make it better?

Anyone who has ever married someone, thinking "After we're married, she'll settle down" or "He'll stop feeling so jealous" knows the answer to that. You can't force a change in someone else's personality.

But if you can't change your child's personality, you *can* learn to understand it and to anticipate the way he or she is likely to react in a given situation. If you know Joanna is somewhat of a loner, you will understand that she may find it difficult to shine in school, where there are so many kids to deal with. If you know she is mild and docile, you won't expect her to run for class president. If you know she is reserved, you won't mistake her lack of hugs and kisses for a lack of love.

And when you understand Joanna, you can be firm when needed, and accept and love her as she is, and help her to be and do *her* best, in *her* way. The natural process of growing up will lead to changes in personality and adjustment that can be blocked by a climate of distress or misunderstanding.

The influential psychologist Erik Erikson, whose thinking has profoundly affected the ideas of many present-day practitioners, divided the development of personality into eight "ages of man." The first three, which occur during the preschool years, are "Autonomy vs. Self-Doubt," "Initiative vs. Guilt," and "Industry vs. Inferiority." In the next few paragraphs, as you watch Jane's personality develop, you will see how these stages evolve and build upon each other.

PERSONALITY FROM AGE THREE TO FIVE

A two-to-three-year-old's proper goal in life is to gain a feeling of autonomy. Jane has to learn that she is a separate individual, not a part of her mother. She has to learn that there is life without Mommy, and indeed that life without Mommy is good! If she doesn't begin to learn this now, she may have trouble letting Mommy go when she starts kindergarten; later in life, if autonomy is still a problem, Jane may be reluctant to leave her parents' home and set up a life of her own.

It is well-known that as a child grows older, his or her willingness to leave Mommy increases. In fact, studies have shown that for each added month of age, a child will travel approximately one foot farther from Mommy's side. Autonomy by the inch!

At two and a half, Jane is eager to do things for herself. She wants to button her own buttons (or try to!), fold her own socks, and get in and out of the car by herself. To the extent that she is permitted to do so, she develops an increased sense of autonomy. "I can do it myself!" is her battle cry.

However, to the extent that Jane's family discourages her from doing things herself ("Let me button that for you, sweetie." "Look at that! You put a red sock with a blue sock. Better let me do it for you"), Jane develops self-doubt.

This stage of personality development is a battle between autonomy and self-doubt, and the child who comes through it with the balance in favor of autonomy will have an easier time developing a sense of self-worth. However, some self-doubt is necessary; Jane must have some idea of her limitations.

During the years from three to five, Jane takes increased enjoyment in initiating activities instead of simply imitating or reacting to the people around her. When she is encouraged to do what she wants to do, when her questions are taken seriously and are given thoughtful answers, and when her imaginative play is encouraged, she will develop initiative. But to the extent that she is discouraged ("No, you can't make a boat, you'll mess up my workshop." "I can't talk about snakes now, I'm busy!" "Janie, you know there's no such thing as dragons! Get serious!"), she will develop a sense of guilt. Again, some sense of guilt is as necessary as initiative, but the well-balanced personality is weighted in favor of initiative rather than guilt.

At six, Jane will enter a period when her personality is acquiring a sense of industry as opposed to a sense of inferiority. Reassurance and praise for her busy, creative activities encourage the former. If she is discouraged too often, however, her sense of inferiority will be strengthened. ("I'm no good at that. I'd just mess it up.")

As their personalities develop, children must learn to regulate conflicting aspects of their personalities (autonomy vs. self-doubt, initiative vs. guilt, industry vs. inferiority) so that they can enjoy life and still have enough of a conscience to control their behavior.

BEHAVIOR RATING SCALE

One of the ways in which personality expresses itself is in behavior. The following test contains a variety of items reflecting several patterns of behavior.

Instructions: Rate your child on each of the items, according to how often you have observed him or her demonstrating that behavior at home and at play, and how often you have received reports of that behavior from teachers. Respond to all of the items. If the item is true most of the time or often, place a check in the "yes" column. If the item is not true most of the time, place a check in the "no" column. Checks in circles indicate *inappropriate* behavior for the age level.

OBSERVING ANXIETY/ANGER

	Age		
	3½ Yes No	4½ Yes No	5½ Yes No
1. Smiles	□ ○	□ ○	□ ○
2. Plays with only one child	□ □	○ □	○ □
3. Hits adults at nursery school	○ □	○ □	○ □
4. Is upset by little things	○ □	○ □	○ □
5. Has many nightmares	○ □	○ □	○ □
6. Plays indoors on sunny days	○ □	○ □	○ □
7. Is afraid of dogs	□ □	○ □	○ □
8. Lies to get out of trouble	□ □	○ □	○ □
9. Likes to run errands	□ ○	□ ○	□ ○
10. Has trouble waking in morning	○ □	○ □	○ □
11. Talks to strangers	□ □	○ □	○ □
12. Feels sorry for himself/herself	○ □	○ □	○ □
13. Needs frequent punishment	○ □	○ □	○ □

(Continued on next page)

	3½ Yes No		4½ Yes No		5½ Yes No	
	_____ *Age* _____					
14. Has many friends	□	□	□	○	□	○
15. Shows off	□	□	○	□	○	□
16. Destroys other children's toys	○	□	○	□	○	□
17. Is afraid of thunder and lightning	□	□	□	□	○	□
18. Often gets up in the night	□	□	○	□	○	□
19. Is cruel to animals	○	□	○	□	○	□
20. Carries a blanket or doll	□	□	○	□	○	□
21. Argues often with his/her friends	○	□	○	□	○	□
22. Wets the bed	□	□	○	□	○	□
23. Clings to familiar adult	○	□	○	□	○	□
24. Accepts babysitter when parents go out	□	□	□	○	□	○
25. Often says negative things about self (e.g., "I'm dumb.")	○	□	○	□	○	□
26. Face shows little expression or feeling	○	□	○	□	○	□
27. Bangs head on floor or walls	○	□	○	□	○	□
28. Blinks or twitches without apparent reason	○	□	○	□	○	□
29. Is afraid of the dark	□	□	○	□	○	□
30. Hits out at others	□	□	○	□	○	□
31. Likes to cuddle	□	○	□	○	□	○

OBSERVING OVERACTIVITY AND INATTENTION

Instructions: Observe your child for a week. Check the appropriate box for each behavior. Checks in solid boxes indicate appropriate behavior for the age level. Checks in the circles indicate inappropriate behavior.

	Age		
	3½ Yes No	4½ Yes No	5½ Yes No
1. Wiggles constantly	□ □	○ □	○ □
2. Inattentive when watching TV	□ □	○ □	○ □
3. Interrupts	□ □	○ □	○ □
4. Listens to stories being read	□ ○	□ ○	□ ○
5. Tries to stay in the lines when coloring	□ □	□ ○	□ ○
6. Tries to tie shoes	□ □	□ ○	□ ○
7. Jumps on furniture	□ □	□ □	□ □
8. Repeatedly asks the same question	□ □	□ ○	○ □
9. Rocks when sitting	○ □	○ □	○ □
10. Tosses toys and laughs repetitively	○ □	○ □	○ □
11. Resists hugs or being held on a lap	○ □	○ □	□ □
12. Goes to sleep early	□ ○	□ ○	□ □
13. Wakes frequently in the night	○ □	○ □	○ □
14. Has a very messy room	□ □	○ □	○ □
15. Builds with blocks or sets up play figures, playing for twenty minutes	□ □	□ ○	□ ○

THE SOCIAL/EMOTIONAL BALANCE

A child's social/emotional status is a complex matter, but it is possible to look at your child's behavior to get some clues about how she feels. The questions below can help you get a feel for your child's social/emotional balance in five different areas.

Five separate scores will be determined from the results of this test, one score for each of the following facets of personality: Warmth/Coolness, Impulse Control/Aggressiveness, Security/Anxiety, Cooperativeness/Uncooperativeness, Sociability/Withdrawal.

Instructions: Look at the overall pattern of answers on the Behavior Rating Scale and decide how you would rate your child in the following areas. Place an X on the line at the point that applies for your child. The high score shows more positive adjustment.

1. WARMTH/COOLNESS

Does the child seem to show emotion easily and interact with others in an outgoing manner?

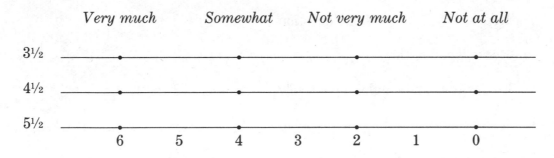

2. IMPULSE CONTROL/AGGRESSIVENESS

Does the child deal with hurt or frustration or conflict in a calm manner?

	Very much	Somewhat	Not very much	Not at all
3½				
4½				
5½				
	6　5	4　3	2　1	0

3. SECURITY/ANXIETY

Does the child seem confident, independent, and comfortable at home and away from home?

	Very much	Somewhat	Not very much	Not at all
3½				
4½				
5½				
	6　5	4　3	2　1	0

4. COOPERATIVENESS/UNCOOPERATIVENESS

Does the child seem eager to please and to go along with others?

	Very much	Somewhat	Not very much	Not at all
3½				
4½				
5½				
	6　5	4　3	2　1	0

(Continued on next page)

5. SOCIABILITY/WITHDRAWAL

Does the child tend to seek the company of other people?

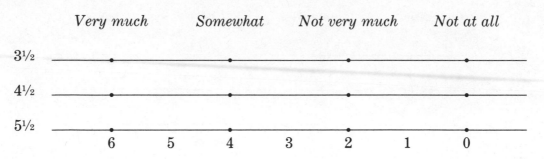

| | Very much | Somewhat | Not very much | Not at all |

3½

4½

5½

6   5   4   3   2   1   0

MAKE A FACE

Instructions: Begin by asking, "Can you make a happy face? Can you make a mad face?" (Demonstrate, if necessary). Then show your child the pictures of faces with feelings. Check off on the list below any feeling the child uses to label the faces. If your child names some not on our list, write them in. For the purposes of this game, any feeling labels should be accepted and checked off, even if you think the face should be labeled with a different feeling. (For general scoring instructions, see pages 45–49.)

1.   2.   3.

 4.

 5.

 6.

 7.

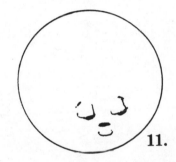 8.

 9.

 10.

 11.

 12.

	Age		
	3½	4½	5½
1. Happy	____	____	____
2. Sad	____	____	____
3. Mad	____	____	____
4. Worried	____	____	____

(Continued on next page)

	Age		
	3½	4½	5½
5. Mean	_____	_____	_____
6. Lonely	_____	_____	_____
7. Sorry	_____	_____	_____
8. Mixed-up	_____	_____	_____
9. Sick	_____	_____	_____
10. Surprised	_____	_____	_____
11. Shy	_____	_____	_____
12. Embarrassed	_____	_____	_____
Other	_____	_____	_____
Other	_____	_____	_____
Other	_____	_____	_____

	Age		
	3½	4½	5½
_____ (Child identifies two or three feelings)	☐	☐	☐
_____ (Child identifies four or five feelings)	☐	☐	☐
_____ (Child identifies six or more feelings)	☐	☐	☐

SOMEONE JUST LIKE ME

This test gives an indication of your child's balance between security and anxiety.

Instructions: Ask your child to draw a picture of someone "just like you." This drawing is not for scoring purposes—it is simply designed as an introduction to the next "personality game." However, it is important that your child understand that this drawing is of someone who is a lot like him or her. To reinforce this idea, begin with the following questions: "If this child is a lot like you, is it a boy or a girl? How many brothers and sisters does he/she have? If he/she is a lot like you, what color hair does he/she have? What color eyes? What is his/her favorite color? What is his/her favorite food?" By this time, you should be able to tell whether your child has identified with the drawing. If your child persistently gives answers that you know are inappropriate—for instance, if your daughter says her drawing is of a ten-year-old boy—do not continue with the rest of the game. Wait until the next age level, and try again.

Once you are sure that your child understands that the drawing is of someone who looks and feels the same way he or she does, go on to the test questions below. In each instance, check the answer your child gives, even though you feel that a different answer would have been closer to the truth.

Place a check in the circle or square after the first part of each question if the answer to that part of the question is "yes." Place a check in the circle or the square after the second part of each question if the answer to that part of the question is "yes." Do not make a check for a "no" answer. For each pair of questions, you will end up with a check in either a circle or a square, but not both.

	Age		
	3½	4½	5½
1. Does the boy/girl talk during Show and Tell . . .	□	□	□
or does he/she feel shy and embarrassed to talk during Show and Tell?	○	○	○

(Continued on next page)

	Age		
	3½	4½	5½
2. Does he/she think he/she has good luck . . .	☐	☐	☐
or does he/she think he/she has bad luck?	○	○	○
3. Do people say bad things about him/her . . .	○	○	○
or do they usually say nice things?	☐	☐	☐
4. Do most people like him/her . . .	☐	☐	☐
or do most people not like him/her?	○	○	○
5. Is he/she afraid of the dark . . .	○	○	○
or is he/she not afraid of the dark?	☐	☐	☐
6. Do most people think he/she is a bad child . . .	○	○	○
or do they think he/she is pretty good?	☐	☐	☐
7. Are his/her dreams mostly happy . . .	☐	☐	☐
or does he/she often have bad dreams?	○	○	○
8. Does it bother him/her when he/she gets cut and bleeds . . .	○	○	○
or doesn't he/she care too much when that happens?	☐	☐	☐
9. Does he/she worry that something bad might happen to him/her or to his/her family . . .	○	○	○
or doesn't he/she think about bad things happening?	☐	☐	☐

	Age		
	3½	4½	5½

10. Does he/she think a lot about
people dying . . .
or does he/she only sometimes
think about dying?

        ○   ○   ○

        □   □   □

11. Does he/she like to play on rainy
days . . .
or do rainy days make him/her
very sad?

        □   □   □

        ○   ○   ○

Scoring: Children with more boxes than circles checked off show less anxiety than children with a number of circles checked off.

WHAT TO DO WITH YOUR RESULTS

It is important to realize in conducting these tests that you are looking for *patterns* of behavior. Therefore, if Joanna has nightmares but shows no other signs of high anxiety, no emotional problem is likely to be involved. (This is not to say that you won't want to search for the cause of the nightmares; it is merely to point out that no pattern of anxiety has been formed yet.)

Also, you are looking for patterns displayed both at home and at school. If Joanna displays a lot of anger—but only at school, not at home or in the neighborhood—it may be a sign, not of a hostile personality, but that she is being bugged by something at school—inability to see the blackboard, for example, leading to frustration expressed in anger. Again, you would want to look into the situation, but you shouldn't take it as a sign that Joanna is generally aggressive. She may just need new glasses.

Our measures are designed to find patterns that suggest that Joanna is carrying a problem, rather than that she is simply having trouble coping with a particular situation. Naturally, when Joanna is having trouble, you want to help. But a single problem doesn't form a pattern that points to personality or social-emotional adjustment problems.

Joanna's *emotional* adjustment reflects the way she feels about herself and her world, how comfortable she is with herself. Her *social* adjustment reflects the way she relates to and gets along with others.

Of course, in real live children, these two areas are so intertwined that trying to separate them is like trying to pick one paper clip out of a boxful—using a magnet. Somehow, a whole lot of other paper clips get involved. So when five-year-old Stan turns every neighborhood game into a prizefight, does this aggressive behavior indicate a problem in getting along with others, or some feeling of insecurity within himself? It could be either or both.

Or if it's an isolated or short-lived situation, it may not indicate a real problem at all. Maybe Stan's father has begun introducing him to the principles of boxing and he's simply practicing on his friends. The important thing is to look for that pattern and not to make any judgments unless and until you have found it.

If Joanna shows up positively on most of our tests and games, she is in good shape. She probably has several good friends and gets along pretty well with all of them, barring the occasional fight that soon blows over. When you ask her to set the table, she might groan or make a face, but she will usually do it. When you give her a hug, she will hug back, but she is too busy to sit and cuddle with you in the middle of the day. Sometimes she is generous and sometimes not. And she may have a sad dream that she shares with you in the morning. All of this is normal childhood behavior.

If Joanna scores *very* positively, she is probably mature for her age. If she is high in most or all of the tests you have conducted in this book, she may well be gifted.

What if Joanna demonstrates a number of negative emotions on our tests? She may just need to grow up a little bit. If she has problems with friends, a few more months or a year of playing with other children her age may help her to understand what kind of behavior is acceptable to other kids. In other words, she will figure out for herself that if you hit your friend with a truck too often, he won't want to come over and play with you. Nursery school may be helpful here. Exposure to a group of active playmates will speed the process of learning to relate to others.

If Joanna scores high in anxiety, she may be going through a period in which she will need some guidance and support and understanding. It may be enough for you simply to be aware of her feelings of insecurity, or you may want to discuss it with your child's teachers and/or pediatrician. If the situation doesn't clear up in a reasonable amount of time or if it seems to be getting worse instead of better, the school or doctor may refer you to a psychologist.

If you do feel concern over Joanna's personality adjustment, begin with the nursery school and the pediatrician. After your general opening question, focus on any areas that are of concern to you: "Does Joanna seem to handle anger well at school? How does she get along with her friends here?" The teacher should be able to help you determine whether Joanna is going through a temporary bad time, perhaps caused by stress at home or at school, or whether it might be wise for you to seek professional help. Public schools, with their preschool screening programs for children about to enter kindergarten, may be able to offer further information about Joanna's adjustment. And both the school and your pediatrician will be able to refer you to a psychologist.

Another route would be to go directly to a psychologist or child guidance clinic. This is a time when the advice and information of family and friends can be helpful. Find out if anyone you know has consulted a child psychologist. Were they satisfied? What was the psychologist like? Were they comfortable with him or her? How did he or she relate to their children?

It's legitimate to shop around for a psychologist. You want to be comfortable with the doctor, to feel free to discuss feelings and situations that may be difficult to talk about.

Once you have located a practitioner you have confidence in, he or she will observe and test Joanna to form a diagnosis. Thereafter, there are two kinds of approaches that can be used to help improve your child's situation. One is direct intervention—meetings with the child alone. The other approach involves the parents as well as the child.

Techniques that involve the parents include family therapy, counseling of the parents alone, or participation in one of the many parenting programs that are offered by schools and other community organizations.

These groups offer support that can be very helpful. When a child is undergoing emotional stress, the parents cannot help being stressed as well, either as a result of the child's problem or as part of the cause—in a divorce, for example. Support for the parent can create a lessening of strain for both parents and children and can help to renew everyone's sense of personal worth.

Each child is an individual. Not every child is headed for the same place, any more than every family goes to Yellowstone for summer vacation, so the same track won't work for all children. Helping your Brian to find the right track is part of knowing him.

Of course, *complete* understanding of your child is an impossible dream. But we hope that through the games and tests in this book, you will come to know your child a little better. We hope, too, that you'll see that *understanding* is the goal. The reason for trying to understand Brian is not so that you can "fix" him if something goes wrong—although of course you would want to help him as much as you could. The real reason is to better love and live with the complex, contradictory, unique little stranger who shares your life.

□APPENDIX A□

Case Histories and Conclusions

It bears repeating: Your child is not simply a set of skills labeled "motor," "language," "self-help," and so on. Your child is a person—an entity with feelings and ideas and abilities you may never be able to fathom entirely. Indeed, how could you? From the moment Sarah is conceived, her chemistry and her life experiences differ from yours, creating a special person. The fact that she would not exist without you does not mean that you will instinctively understand her. It takes patience and effort to get along with your child, just as it does to get along with your husband, your wife, your employer—even your own parents.

Another fact also bears repeating: No two children are the same. Sarah likes numbers and concrete facts; Brian likes to create fantasy worlds; Susan is outgoing and gregarious; Janine is more comfortable with adults than with children; Roger likes to take things apart and put them back together; Terry was reading by age four; Ellen is sure to be an artist when she grows up. It would be outrageous to expect all these children to become newspaper editors, or corporate executives, or science teachers.

The uniqueness of each child can be especially clear after a day in a professional counselor's office. Meet Jason, Kendra, Bobby, Mimi, Joanna, Jennifer, Carl, Jamie, Paolo, and Dwayne—ten children whose only similarity is that they have all come to the same counselor for help in dealing with problems that are—or may be—interfering with their progress.

Jason

For the first three years of his life, Jason was a happy, outgoing, pleasant child. However, when his younger brother was born and his older sister went off to public school, Jason's personality seemed to undergo a change. He became cranky and uncooperative, and was often ill. His language skills fell noticeably behind those of his peers. His nursery-school teacher noticed that he seemed withdrawn, and that he often lashed out at his playmates without cause. When he turned five, his parents were uncertain whether to put him in kindergarten or give him another year of nursery school.

Preplacement assessment at the local school indicated that Jason was well able to cope with school; however, tests indicated the possibility of a hearing problem. After some delay and lack of communication between Jason's parents and the school, Jason was taken to a hearing specialist, and was diagnosed as having a hearing problem, caused by the series of colds and ear infections he had had starting at the age of three. An operation remedied the physical problem with his hearing, and special counseling at school helped Jason to relate better with his peers.

Unlike Jason, Kendra experienced setbacks right from the start.

Kendra

Kendra's complications began before she was born. Her mother suffered from diabetes and became severely undernourished during her pregnancy. Kendra was delivered by Caesarean section at seven and a half months—a delivery further complicated by obstetric difficulties. In spite of her premature birth, she weighed six pounds, thirteen ounces. However, she lacked the sucking reflex and had to spend her first week in intensive care.

She was frequently ill with colds during her first year. Although she was an active child, her parents noticed that her strength and coordination lagged behind other children's. She did not begin to walk until sixteen months, and although she began speaking at eight months, her

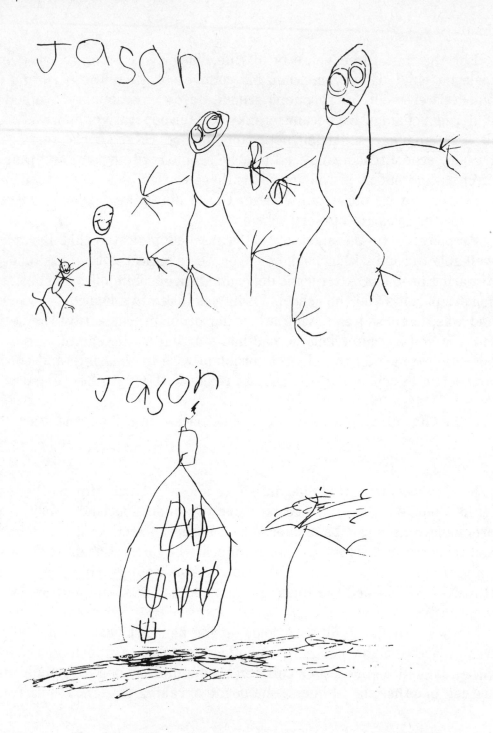

ABCDEFGHIJKLMNOPQRSTUVW
XYZ

1 2 3 4 5 6 7 8 9 10 11 12 13 14
15 16 17 18 19 20 21 22 23 24
25 26 27 28 29 30 31 32 33

The drawings of Jason Evans reflect both his capability and his distress. The pictures are quite detailed and complete. But there is a stressed quality as well. The double-circled eyes and the long fingers give a jangled look. The windows on the house are heavily crossed; the crosses extend beyond the frames. The psychologist would look to other tests for more signs of a sense of pressure and difficulty with controls in such a child to determine whether these signs are corroborated.

speech development was inconsistent. Her mother felt that Kendra took after her father, who had had significant speech and coordination problems as a child.

When she was three and a half, Kendra began nursery school, where her slow development quickly became obvious. Her speech was so unintelligible that her teacher suggested testing her for hearing loss. However, no such loss was found.

At five and a half, Kendra seemed to be functioning on the level of a four-year-old, playing alone most of the time and joining the other children only in directed activities. Her parents were thoroughly confused by their child's inconsistent behavior: sometimes she seemed to catch on quickly, and sometimes she seemed confused. Was Kendra mentally retarded?

Evaluation showed that she was not. In fact, her intelligence was above average, but she was suffering from a broad developmental delay caused by her early physical problems. It was like hitting the pause button on a tape player—she was held back each time she was ill, and she had never caught up. Kendra was given language therapy, and by the time she entered second grade, she was ready for placement with an average group of students.

Kendra's parents, like many others, feared that their child's problems suggested retardation. Kendra's serious early growing setbacks had heightened their fears.

Bobby's parents, by contrast, were sure their son was bright, even though he showed some of the same traits that were characteristic of Kendra: anxiety and a reserved personality. Nevertheless, they still had some questions that could only be answered by a professional.

Bobby

Bobby was a pleasant, outgoing five-year-old whose parents thought he was quite bright. However, at times he seemed to be trying too hard, and he became tongue-tied when he felt too much pressure. His parents were unsure whether to have him spend a second year in kindergarten

Kendra's drawings reflect her immaturity. By five and a half, almost all children will include a body in a drawing of a person; Kendra did not. Attaching the arms to the head is a further indication that Kendra was developmentally delayed. On the other hand, the presence of facial features, ears, hair, and toes shows that her development was emerging. Overall, Kendra's drawings also show that she hesitated to put a lot of herself into her work.

or go on to the first grade. They were certain that he was smart enough to keep up, but they worried that the pressure might be too much for him. When the kindergarten teacher suggested counseling, they were reluctant, thinking that they didn't really need professional help; however, they decided to try it.

They felt much better after formal testing revealed that Bobby's IQ was 147—very high. Although the developmental and personality tests revealed that Bobby had a serious and somewhat anxious side, it was decided that his parents' concern was unnecessary, and Bobby went on to first grade, gaining confidence and meeting with good success.

Bobby's insecurity stemmed from his temperament and his high self-expectations. His family was basically secure, and both parents viewed their responsibilities as parents in a similar light. For them, counseling did not seem indicated.

It was a different matter for Mimi, whose insecurity and anger were caused by severe disruptions in her life. She had all the more difficulty in dealing with these problems because her parents each gave her very different messages about what was happening. Her problem required both individual and family counseling.

Mimi

Mimi's parents were divorced. Her mother felt that there was no cause for concern in Mimi's behavior, but her father was disturbed, and when Mimi came to visit him, he brought her in for an assessment.

Bobby's drawings reflect both his brightness and some of his anxiety. The sun with a face and the bird in flight convey ideas and awarenesses more typical of an older child. The drawing of the person beside the house, on the other hand, is noteworthy for the poor connection between head and body. This might indicate Bobby's uncertainty about putting his mental abilities together with the rest of himself. A psychologist would, of course, look for more evidence of this than is shown in one drawing alone.

Mimi had difficulty adjusting to school. She disliked her teachers, whom she claimed scolded and embarrassed her. Her behavior toward other children tended to be violent and aggressive, particularly when she failed to get her own way. She was fearful, refusing to be left alone in any part of the house and not wanting to go into a dark room. She did not like to sleep alone.

Mimi's parents needed a better way to record their daughter's behavior to discover what patterns might be forming, and they also needed a more effective way of communicating with each other. If they had been more successful in observing and talking together about Mimi's difficulties, many of the problems might have been detected sooner, to Mimi's advantage.

Counseling and therapy were initiated for Mimi and for her parents.

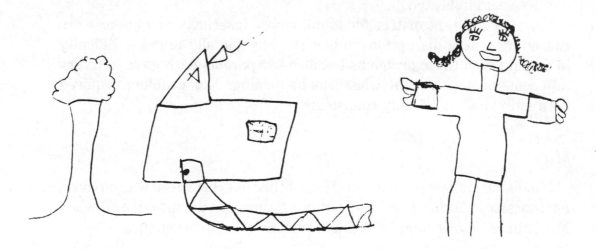

Mimi's picture shows subtle signs of distress. The little girl she drew lacks a smiling, comfortable expression. The path to the house is criss-crossed—perhaps difficult to walk along. However, the psychologist would look for other indications that Mimi was uncomfortable before coming to a firm conclusion. Mimi's attention to eye detail might suggest that she felt a need to be vigilant, or it might suggest her concern with how she looked to others. More confirmation would be gathered from other tests to make a complete description of Mimi.

This led to improved communication between the parents and more security for the child, whose behavior began to show improvement.

Like Mimi, Joanna's parents were divorced. But another dimension was added to her problems.

Joanna

Joanna was a six-year-old who had been removed from her parents; they had neglected and physically abused her. She lived with her grandmother. She was an alert child of average intellectual ability (IQ 101) who was doing well in school. Her drawing reveals that she viewed her family as herself and her grandmother but felt that something was missing. She filled in the missing element by adding the "bunny" on the TV screen.

Joanna was not in serious trouble emotionally, but her past history suggested that a short-term program of play therapy would help her continue her healing process and would help keep the sadness and emptiness she felt from having an impact on her developing personality. Counseling was provided with services paid under a state medical funding program.

It isn't always problems that send families to the psychologist's office, as Jennifer's parents know.

Jennifer

Just before Jennifer entered kindergarten, her parents were interested in finding out how she was doing. There was no particular problem to be dealt with; they simply wanted to learn about her fund of information and to get a baseline from which they could gauge her future progress.

Tests showed Jennifer to be delightfully average. Her fund of information was typical of most children her age; she had a good knowledge

Joanna's broken family may mean that essential affection and nurturing were missing from her life. While this is not always the case, for Joanna we may suspect the lack, because without being asked to, she left something out of her family picture—her mother, father, and siblings—and added something else—the bunny. The soft, cuddly bunny may be a substitute for the soft nurturing Joanna needs. It is a TV bunny, however, not a real, warm, living bunny. A psychologist would want to be alert for other signs of possible affectional deprivation.

of the world around her for a four-and-a-half-year-old, and she interacted well with the examiner, showing no unusual signs of shyness and being perfectly willing to initiate conversations. Her success in nursery school had prepared her for a successful adjustment to the public school system, and the examiner predicted a good school year for Jennifer.

Jennifer's drawings show the happy and well-adjusted child indicated by her other measures. Her drawings are well developed, with appropriate detail. The figures show age- and role-appropriate movement: the smallest child in a swing and the older children playing a game. The drawing of a single person is smiling and is a girl, the same as Jennifer, showing clear sex-role identification.

Unlike Jennifer, Carl did have a problem—one that his family acknowledged and was coping with. However, professional advice and counseling did help the family to answer a question they had been asking themselves.

Carl

Like many mildly retarded children, Carl was a charmer. He was so charming, in fact, that people tended to respond to him in ways that were appropriate for a child much younger than his real age of six and a half.

Carl was doing well in his special-education classes, although his speech was often unintelligible. His vocabulary was appropriate for a child half his age. He was physically adept, and he got along well with his friends. During the summer, Carl joined in a swimming program at the YMCA with normal boys of his age, and to his mother's pleasure, he did very well. Surely, if he got on well with children his age, he was ready to follow a normal school program?

Although Carl did not seem retarded in many ways, his language problem was a clue to his developmental limitation. Language problems are often tied in to a more general learning problem. By including some mainstreaming in Carl's school program, educators were able to move him along toward greater social maturity. However, special education programming was necessary to address Carl's special learning needs in communication.

Carl was six and a half, and his drawing is a bit like Kendra's. Remember, however, that Kendra was five and a half, and her drawing is like one of an even younger child—perhaps three or three and a half. Thus, Carl's drawing shows more than a little immaturity. In Carl's case, the drawing is consistent with slow development. The house, tree, and person are distorted, not simply by his lack of ability to draw but by the difficulty Carl had in getting a mental concept of these common items. Even when the model was partially supplied, as in the "What's Missing?" picture, Carl had difficulty adding the details. His motor control and body awareness were also limited.

Carl's language difficulties signaled slow development and mental retardation. By contrast, Jamie's language difficulties were combined with
better-than-average intelligence. Both children showed social maturity
difficulties, but the basis was different, and so the programs selected to
help the two were different. Special education with partial mainstreaming was fine for Carl; Jamie required something else.

Jamie

Jamie displayed speech difficulties, was physically awkward, and seemed
to lack control over his body; he had difficulty playing with other children,
becoming overexcited and unable to control his impulses. He had trouble
listening to spoken directions and was often unable to center his attention
on the person who was speaking to him. His mother was concerned that
he might have some hearing and visual problems, and that he might be
learning disabled.

Tests showed that his intelligence was above average. Hints of difficulties with auditory and visual reasoning tasks appeared on the tests,
but because he was still barely four, it was decided to re-evaluate these
areas in six months to a year. Meanwhile, he was placed with a school
group of three- to four-year-olds rather than with four- to five-year-olds,
and he was given speech and language therapy.

Upon re-evaluation a year later, it was found that Jamie's speech
difficulties were being worked out. However, his intellectual capacities
were not being carried over into the social and emotional areas. The
examiner concluded that Jamie was probably not ready for a full kindergarten program with the prospect of first grade a year after. Instead,
because he needed to have lower expectations and more time to grow,
it was recommended that he attend a kindergarten-nursery school for
five-year-olds.

For many children, growth problems are not physically demonstrated
but manifest themselves through problems in development in other areas.
For Paolo, however, an obvious physical difference from the norm did
exist, along with hidden maturity factors.

Jamie's drawings suggest several possibilities. His drawing of a person suggests that he may have been feeling less than adequate in dealing with things in his life. The lack of arms often indicates a feeling of lack of power. The numbers suggest that Jamie was being taught a skill before he was ready. He drew them incorrectly and lacked a good concept of their form or function. Perhaps Jamie was being pushed a bit by his parents and felt still more inadequate as a result.

Paolo

Paolo was a small child, a condition caused by a low level of growth hormone. His birth and development were normal, but his coordination lagged somewhat; at the age of five, he could not skip or tie his shoes. He tended to become irritable when he was tired.

Paolo's parents were concerned. Because he was small and not well coordinated, they reasoned, wouldn't it be better to hold him back in kindergarten for one more year before sending him to first grade?

After observing and testing Paolo, his psychologist agreed that it would be a good idea to wait a year to give Paolo's nervous system some

Paolo's coordination problems and small size were not reflected in his happy and imaginative drawings. Clearly, Paolo's world of fantasy was available to make up for some of what he lacked physically.

extra time to mature, so that he would have a little extra control to meet the demands of school.

It was a wise decision. Although schools are always aware of individual students, and understand that each child has special needs, they are not well equipped to help those who are "more different" than the average. With the extra year under his belt, Paolo was close enough to "normal" to handle school fairly well.

Paolo and the children described so far have all coped fairly well in spite of their difficulties. Dwayne, however, represents a more extreme situation. While divorce had meant anger and confusion for Mimi, it became a part of a far more serious set of problems for Dwayne.

Dwayne

Dwayne was just too much for his mother to handle. In fact, he was too big a handful for his nursery school, too. The school solved the problem by expelling him; his mother didn't have that option.

Dwayne's birth and early years were normal, but his parents had separated before he was born, so Dwayne never lived with his father. His mother admitted that she let him get away with murder. He fought constantly with his brother, and when he didn't get his own way, he screamed. He was not good at games. His mother thought this was because he wouldn't take the time to learn or let anyone show him anything. He refused to share and was often physically abusive to other children.

At about the age of three, Dwayne began to lose skills that he had previously gained. He was no longer consistent in toilet training, and he had trouble getting to sleep at night. He seemed to require tremendous amounts of help from his mother in dressing and other self-help skills.

When he turned five, it was time to start thinking about kindergarten. But how could he function in a school environment when he couldn't get along with other children or dress himself without help?

Preschool evaluation established that Dwayne was dealing with a serious degree of emotional disturbance. He required a program that would teach him social, emotional, and self-help skills, and his mother needed help in learning to be a consistent and instructive parent. A "family

Dwayne's substantial problems were clearly reflected in his drawings. A scrambled vision of house, tree, and person mirror his disturbed view of himself and his world. It is clear that Dwayne would be unable to handle the demands placed upon him and would require a great deal of help from others.

school," run as part of the community mental health center, provided a combined school and treatment program for Dwayne and counseling for his mother. There, Dwayne developed enough security to move ahead with his self-help skills.

Severe misbehavior along with a virtual stoppage of the normal maturing process were combined in Dwayne, so he required the full-time help of both counseling and a treatment school program.

□APPENDIX B□

Tests

The tests in this appendix are those that are frequently used in evaluating preschool children. Tests included in this listing meet the following criteria: they are standardized, they appear to have good reliability and validity (see chapter 2), and they are widely accepted by professionals who work with young children.

This appendix is intended to provide only a sampling of screening and assessment instruments and is not intended to be all-inclusive.

Norm-Referenced Screening Instruments

The *Comprehensive Identification Process*, given to children aged two and a half to five and a half years old, is used in screening a child's abilities in cognitive, motor, language and speech, and behavior areas. It is also used to test vision and hearing, and it provides for a review of the child's medical and developmental milestones.

The *Denver Developmental Screening Test* can be administered from birth to six years of age. It is used to screen the child's personal-social, language, and motor areas of development.

Developmental Indicators for the Assessment of Learning is an instrument that can be given to children from two and a half to five and a half years of age. The areas screened are gross motor skills, fine motor skills, concepts, and communication.

Criterion-Referenced Assessment Instruments

These tests are "normative" referenced: They contain items in which developmental skills are assigned developmental ages.

The *Brigance Diagnostic Inventory of Early Development*, which can be administered from birth to age seven, assesses the child's skills in psychomotor abilities, self-help, communication, general knowledge, reading, printing, and mathematics.

The *Learning Accomplishment Profile*, given from one month to six years of age, assesses motor, self-help, cognitive, language, and social skills.

The *Portage Guide to Early Education* may be given from birth to age six. It is used in evaluating infant stimulation, socialization, and self-help, language, cognition, and motor skills.

Norm-Referenced Assessment Instruments

The following instruments provide norms for children under the age of six.

The *Bayley Scales of Infant Development* are administered from birth to thirty months. Two scales are included: mental and motor. The mental scale measures early acquisition of object constancy and memory, learning and problem-solving ability, the beginning of verbal communication, and early indications of the ability to form generalizations and classifications. The motor scale measures the degree of control of the body, plus gross and fine motor coordination. An Infant Behavior Record is also included, which deals with social orientation and emotional variables, plus a general evaluation.

The *McCarthy Scales of Children's Abilities*, administered from two and a half to eight and a half years, consist of six scales, including verbal, perceptual, quantitative, memory, motor, and general cognitive.

The *Wechsler Preschool and Primary Scale of Intelligence*, administered to children from four to six and a half years of age, is a downward extension of the Wechsler Intelligence Scale for Children, a frequently used scale for school-aged IQ testing. Scaled scores for a verbal and a performance section are obtained. Verbal scales are for Information, Vocabulary, Arithmetic, Similarities, and Comprehension. Performance scales include Animal House (visual-motor sequencing), Picture Completion, Mazes, Geometric Design, and Block Design.

Glossary

Many of the terms included in this glossary will be found in the text; others are presented for the first time, but you *may* hear them in the office of the pediatrician, the psychologist, or the school principal.

Achievement—Actual performance. Used in reference to test scores and school performance.

Achievement test—A measure of a child's level of proficiency or performance in a given area or field.

Active listening—A way of encouraging children to solve problems by themselves. It requires that the adult listen to the child's feelings in a nonjudgmental way and accurately feed back the feelings to the child.

Adjustment—The relationship between the motivated person and the environment.

Aggression—Behavior that is hurtful, destructive, or demeaning to others.

Anxiety—A diffuse, unfocused, and vaguely perceived emotional state characterized by apprehension, tension, or uneasiness.

Aphasia—A language disturbance, usually caused by brain damage; may be sensory, motor, or both.

Aptitude—Potential capacity to learn, as inferred from performance.

Assertiveness—Behavior that is a statement of one's rights in a way that is not hurtful, destructive, or demeaning to others.

Attention deficit disorder—A condition in which the child displays signs of inattention, impulsiveness, and hyperactivity that are inappropriate for his/her age.

Attitude—Readiness to behave in a consistent way toward a given object or type of object.

Auditory—Pertaining to hearing.

Authoritarian parenting—A parenting style characterized by the imposition of many rules and in which the child is given little freedom. The parent makes *all* the decisions.

Authoritative parenting—A parenting style characterized by the parents' clearly communicating to the child their expectations regarding behavior. Firm controls are exercised, yet these controls are not repressive. The parents also allow the child to make certain developmentally appropriate decisions.

Autism—A developmental disability caused by a physical disorder of the brain. Symptoms include disturbances in physical, social, and language skills; abnormal responses to sensations; and abnormal ways of relating to people, objects, and events.

Autistic thinking—Thinking that is determined primarily by the individual's needs or desires; daydreaming.

Behavior modification—A way of modifying observable behavior by offering rewards for acceptable behavior and punishment of nonacceptable behavior.

Coercive discipline—The use of physical or psychological force or threats to cause behavioral changes.

Concept—Idea or conclusion based on a generalization.

Conditioning—Learning in which a new stimulus generates an old response, such as salivating (response) at the sound of a bell (stimulus).

Conflict—The stress involved when one is motivated by incompatible needs or tendencies.

Consequences, natural and logical—Those consequences, or natural results of an action, that permit children to learn from the natural order of the physical world and from the reality of the social order.

Consistency—Displaying the same reaction each time a given behavior occurs. An adult's consistency in reacting to a child's behavior reduces the child's tendency to test the limits of permissible behavior. Inconsistent performance is less effective in stopping inappropriate behavior than is consistent punishment. In addition, when two adults are inconsistent with each other in dealing with a child's inappropriate behavior, there is less chance that the behavior will change than if the adults are consistent.

Defense mechanism—A reaction to frustration or conflict that defends the person against anxiety. "I don't care" is a common one.

Developmental—Having to do with the normal sequence in which a child grows and matures.

Diagnostic test—One designed to discover and describe the nature of emotional or behavioral problems.

Echolalia—Parrotlike repetition of sounds.

Ego—The concept of *self*. In psychoanalytic theory, the rational, problem-solving part of the personality.

Egocentrism—A common preschool characteristic. It refers to the difficulty a child has in looking at the world from someone else's point of view. Children tend rather to overgeneralize their own feelings and experiences.

Elective mutism—A condition in which the child refuses to speak in almost all social situations, despite the ability to speak and to understand spoken language.

Emotion—A complex response involving conscious experience and both internal and external physical responses; fear, love, anger, and the like.

Encopresis—A condition in which, from no physical cause, the child repeatedly has bowel movements in places inappropriate for that purpose.

Encouragement—The process of focusing on the child's assets and strengths in order to build self-confidence and feelings of worth.

Eneuresis—A condition in which the child repeatedly and involuntarily urinates after an age at which bladder control is expected, with no physical cause.

Feedback—Returned information about the consequences of a behavior or an event. Can be internal (from the body) or external (from the behavior of others).

Frustration—The blockage or interference with ongoing motivated behavior, making satisfaction impossible.

Hyperkinetic syndrome—A disorder characterized by overactivity, restlessness, distractibility, short attention span, and difficulties in learning and in perceptual motor function.

Id—The primitive, instinctive part of the personality.

Infantile autism—A disorder characterized by a lack of responsiveness to other people, by gross impairments in communicative skills, and by bizarre responses to various aspects of the environment. The condition develops within the first thirty months of age.

Intelligence—Mental ability, as indicated in terms of task performance, verbal comprehension, reasoning, numerical ability, and other factors.

Intelligence quotient (IQ)—A measure of intelligence based on the ratio of mental age to chronological age.

Learning—Relatively permanent changes in behavior that result from past experience.

Learning disability—A condition in which it is determined that the student has all of the following: (1) a measured, severe discrepancy between educational performance and measured intellectual ability; (2) inadequate processing skills; (3) adequate motivation to learn, and (4) no identifiable handicapping conditions or situational trauma that could account for the student's level of functioning. Note that specific definitions may vary somewhat in schools from state to state, but they all generally include the criteria stated.

Maturation—Development based on hereditary factors as opposed to that based on learning.

Mental retardation—The slowing or repressing of intellectual development.

Neonate—Newborn infant.

Neurologist—A physician with postgraduate training and experience in the field of organic diseases of the nervous system.

Norm—A standard against which individual performance can be quantitatively assessed.

Objectivity—In psychological testing, the degree to which two people can score a subject's answers and get the same results.

Oppositional disorder—A condition in which a child exhibits a pattern of disobedient, negativistic, and provoking opposition to authority figures, without, however, violating basic rights of others or deviating excessively from behavior considered appropriate for his/her peer group.

Overanxious disorder—A condition in which a child exhibits excessive worrying and fearful behavior that is not focused on a specific situation or object.

Parent Effectiveness Training (PET)—A program of child guidance that teaches adults specific skills though which they can communicate acceptance to a child. A central concept in PET is that the use of power-assertive tactics by adults fails to demonstrate acceptance of the child and may actually block the child's ability to change.

Perception—The process of discriminating, differentiating, observing, and understanding data.

Performance test—One emphasizing nonverbal responses.

Personality—The integration of an individual's attitudes, interests, behavior patterns, capacities, abilities, and aptitudes, as seen by other people.

Phobia—An excessive and irrational fear.

Pica—The eating of nonfood substances; for example, paint chips, string, and the like.

Plateau—Flat place on a learning curve, reflecting no improvement despite continued practice.

Positive transfer—Swifter learning caused by previous learning in another situation.

Primary mental ability—The abilities that make up general intelligence: spatial, numerical, and reasoning abilities, perceptual speed, and rote memory.

Prosocial Behavior—behavior characterized by cooperation with and helping of others.

Psychiatrist—A licensed physician (M.D.) who specializes in illnesses or disorders affecting mood, behavior, or thought.

Psychiatry—A medical specialty concerned with the diagnosis and treatment of mental illness.

Psychoanalysis—Psychotherapy involving analysis of unconscious and subconscious conflicts and processes.

Psychologist—A specialist in the areas of behavior, learning, emotions, and interrelationships of normal and abnormal individuals or groups.

Psychology—The science of human behavior and human adjustment to the environment.

Psychosis—A severe mental disorder involving dramatic personality changes.

Psychosomatic illness—Physical symptoms produced by mental disturbance.

Psychotherapy—Psychological methods used in treating behavioral disorders.

Punishment—A method of discipline that expresses the power of personal authority. It is associated with threat, and it demands obedience.

Recall—A method of measuring retention of learned material involving reproduction of the learned material.

Recognition—A method of measuring retention in which the subject is required only to recognize rather than recall the correct response.

Reflective listening—*See* **Active listening.**

Reflex—Automatic, unlearned response to stimulus.

Regression—A return to earlier, more childish behavior.

Reinforcement—The rewarding of a correct response.

Reliability—The tendency of a test to agree with itself when repeated in the same circumstances.

Response cost—A disciplinary technique in which inappropriate behavior results in the loss of something; for example, the unsafe use of a bicycle results in the loss of the use of the bike for a period of time.

Scapegoating—A defense mechanism in which aggression is safely displaced to a safe group or class.

Schizoid disorder of childhood—A condition in which the child's capacity to form friendships is severely defective. Children with this disorder are social isolates who are not apparently distressed by their isolation. They are frequently detached from their environment and appear self-absorbed.

Self-esteem—A judgment that one is personally worthy.

Separation anxiety—A condition in which the child suffers excessive nervousness and fear on separation from parents or from familiar settings.

Sibling—A brother or sister.

Sleep terror disorder—A condition in which a child has repeated episodes of abrupt awakening from sleep, usually beginning with a panicky scream. The child shows signs of intense anxiety and is relatively unresponsive to efforts to comfort him.

Social norm—Standards for behavior that are defined and enforced in group situations.

Standardization—Testing a population to obtain norms with which individual scores can be compared.

Stuttering—A condition in which a child frequently repeats or prolongs sounds, syllables, or words or exhibits frequent hesitations that disrupt the flow of speech.

Superego—The "conscience"; the part of the personality that controls behavior.

Systematic Training for Effective Parenting (STEP)—A program of parent education and child guidance in which key concepts include recognizing the differences between "good" parents and responsible parents, encouragement, logical and natural consequences, and listening and communication skills.

Tic—A condition in which the child exhibits recurrent, involuntary, repetitive, rapid, purposeless movements. The condition may be temporary or chronic.

Time out—A disciplinary technique in which the child is taken from a situation where reinforcers for undesirable behavior are present and is moved to a situation where reinforcers are unavailable.

Tourette's syndrome—A tic involving both physical and vocal manifestations—that is, involuntary repetition of sounds or words.

Trait—A group of behaviors that occur together and make up an enduring character attribute.

Validity—The capacity of a test to measure what it was intended to measure.

Selected Bibliography

Ames, Louise B., and Joan Ames Chase. *Don't Push Your Preschooler*. New York: Harper & Row, 1981.

Brazelton, T. Berry, M.D. *Toddlers and Parents*. New York: Delacorte Press, 1974.

Briggs, Dorothy C. *Your Child's Self Esteem*. New York: Doubleday, 1970.

Dodson, Fitzhugh. *How to Father*. Los Angeles: Nash Publishing Corp., 1974.

————. *How to Parent*. New York: New American Library, 1973.

Fraiberg, Selma H. *The Magic Years*. New York: Charles Scribner's Sons, 1984.

Frank, Joseph. *Children and TV*. New York: Public Affairs Pamphlets.

Gesell, Arnold, and Frances Ilg. *The Child from Five to Ten*. New York: Harper & Row, 1977.

Ginott, Haim. *Between Parent and Child*. New York: Avon, 1969.

Gordon, Ira. *Child Learning Through Child Play*. New York: St. Martin's Press, 1972.

Hymes, James L., Jr. *A Child Development Point of View*. Westport, Conn.: Greenwood Press, 1977.

————. *Teaching the Child Under Six*. Columbus, Ohio: Charles E. Merrill Publishing Co., 1981.

Ilg, Frances, and Louise Bates Ames. *Child Behavior*. New York: Harper & Row, 1982.

Lanes, Selma. *Down the Rabbit Hole*. New York: Atheneum, 1971.

Larrick, Nancy. *A Parent's Guide to Children's Reading*. New York: Doubleday, 1975.

Le Shan, Eda J. *Natural Parenthood*. New York: Signet Books, 1970.

Marzolo, Jean. *Learning Through Play*. New York: Harper & Row, 1974.

Mussen, Paul, et al. *Child Development and Personality*. New York: Harper & Row, 1984.

Salk, Dr. Lee. *What Every Child Would Like His Parents to Know*. New York: Simon & Schuster, 1984.

Shiller, Jack, M.D. *Childhood Illness*. New York: Stein & Day, 1973.

Stant, Margaret A. *The Young Child*. Englewood Cliffs, N.J.: Prentice-Hall, 1972.

Sutton-Smith, Brian and Shirley. *How to Play With Your Children*. New York: Random House, 1974.

Index